the ULTIMATE BOOK of MODERN JUICING

More than 200 Fresh Recipes to Cleanse, Cure, and Keep you Healthy

MIMI KIRK

PHOTOGRAPHS BY MIKE MENDELL

Countryman Press
New York, NY

PHOTOGRAPHS
Mike Mendell unless otherwise indicated:

Page 15: © Creativestock/iStockphoto.com; 17: © michele213/iStockphoto.com; 26: © tashka2000/iStockphoto.com; 32: © letty17/iStockphoto.com; 38: © Kisa_Markiza/iStockphoto.com; 40: © AwakenedEye/iStockphoto.com; 42: © jacktheflipper/iStockphoto.com; 45: © Saturated/iStockphoto.com; © c12/iStockphoto.com; 48: © missaigong/iStockphoto.com; © Rena-Marie/iStockphoto.com; 51: © duckycards/iStockphoto.com; 178: Adventure_Photo/iStockphoto.com; 183: belchonock/iStockphoto.com; 189: © GrenouilleFilms/iStockphoto.com; 192: © Beornbjorn/iStockphoto.com; 196: © hannahmillerick/iStockphoto.com; 200: © TeQui0/iStockphoto.com; 213: © olvas/iStockphoto.com; 225: © KenWiedemann/iStockphoto.com; 231: © MARCELOKRELLING/iStockphoto.com; 288: © RyanJLane/iStockphoto.com; 295: © Liesel_Fuchs/iStockphoto.com

COVER DESIGN
LeAnna Weller Smith

BOOK DESIGN AND LAYOUT
Nick Caruso & Donald Zeilman

ILLUSTRATION
Carolyn Kelly

THE COUNTRYMAN PRESS
43 Lincoln Corners Way
P.O. Box 748, Woodstock, VT 05091

DISTRIBUTED BY
W. W. Norton & Company, Inc.,
500 Fifth Avenue, New York, NY 10110

Printed in the United States

The Ultimate Book of Modern Juicing
978-1-58157-260-5

10   9   8   7   6   5   4   3   2   1

*to all those who believe
health is wealth!*

CONTENTS

· · · · · · · · · · · · · · · · · ·

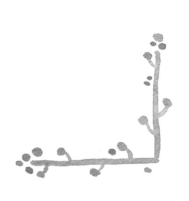

the **ULTIMATE BOOK** of
MODERN JUICING

About the Author

I became a vegetarian in my early 30s and started following a path to enhance my life, which consisted of meditation, personal growth workshops, and practicing mindfulness. I have spent decades researching and practicing natural health to balance mind, body, and spirit.

At the age of 70, I won the title of Sexiest Vegetarian Over 50 in a nationwide contest conducted by PETA, People for the Ethical Treatment of Animals. I'm the best-selling author of *Live Raw: Raw Food Recipes for Good Health and Timeless Beauty* and *Live Raw Around the World*. I'm a certified raw food chef, international speaker, coach, and consultant; and I have a series of YouTube videos demonstrating plant-based food preparation. I was born in 1938, and being healthy at the age of 76 has allowed me to keep up with my rigorous schedule. I do not feel old.

Many people my age not only feel elderly but need daily assistance because of poor health. My good health is not a product of my family's health history, which is not so great. Two of my sisters had cancer and one of them had additional thyroid issues, kidney disease, and diabetes. Another sister died of a heart attack at the age of 55. My brother died from leukemia at the age of 29, and my father had diabetes and Parkinson's disease with complications from these illnesses. He died in his mid-60s. My mother lived long but had heart problems, strokes, arthritis, high blood pressure, and high cholesterol. This is just a portion of my family's health issues. I knew early on that I didn't want to follow in my family's footsteps in regard to health, so that is what put me on the path to researching and finding out what options I had. I would not say that I possess good genes, but because I work on keeping myself healthy, I have so far defeated the health issues that have appeared.

Juicing is a passion of mine. I started juicing in the early 1970s, way before juicing was cool. In the early days, juicers were difficult to clean. After several months of juicing, I would stop juicing daily and only pull out the juicer when my body felt like it needed a little boost. After a few months off from juicing, I would remember how good I felt when I was juicing, so I would start back up again and stay with it for long periods of time. But still, I was not as diligent as I could have been.

I was in my 60s when my doctor told me that my blood pressure and cholesterol level were elevated. I also started feeling arthritic pains in my joints. My doctor said they were just "age-related diseases." I got serious about juicing again, and now, many years later, I can attest that juicing has reversed my health issues. Six months after my doctor handed me the (unfilled) prescription, my blood pressure was back to normal and so was my cholesterol. I've not had an arthritic pain since. All my ailments are gone! Juicing makes me feel healthier and look younger. Juicing changed my life, and I believe it can and has changed many other lives. It works!

Even if you have no interest in changing your standard diet, juicing can improve your health. I have helped many clients begin a healthy lifestyle by encouraging them to change just one thing, and that one thing is adding green juice to their daily diet. Juicing helped them feel better and helped remedy their many illnesses. Encouraged, many of these individuals then took the next step and stopped eating many of the bad foods that had been making them sick and tired.

Juicing has been a wonderful healthy journey for me and my loved ones. I hope this book will be an introduction to healthier habits for you and your loved ones too.

Enjoying a balanced life includes juicing, a healthy diet, meditation, sleep, exercise, being in nature, and love—including self-love.

You can see more information about me on my website, YoungOnRawFood.com.

—Mimi Kirk, January, 2015

INTRODUCTION

Don't ignore your health in search of wealth.

Sure we all love our venti, no sugar, chocolate mocha, 2 percent, double-shot morning habit, but believe it or not we currently live in a juice generation, and one day juice bars will outnumber chain coffee shops like Starbucks. Celebrities and health conscious people have a secret weapon, and it's moving faster than the speed of light. Can you say, 16-ounce apple lemon spinach double ginger with turmeric?

If you don't know much about juicing, let's get you up to speed on its benefits. The food we put in our mouth determines the health of every cell and organ in our body. Food can either help us or do us harm. Juicing is the best way to get the full amount of nutrients and vitamins we need on a daily basis to keep us healthy. Freshly pressed organic vegetable and fruit juice is what we are talking about, not store-bought bottled juices—including orange and apple—or the processed varieties you find on supermarket shelves or in the cooler section.

Juicing is not new to this decade; it has been around for a long time. But juicing trends are showing up in major cities and fashionable hip neighborhoods around the country. Guess who is up to speed on juicing? Bill Clinton, Jennifer Aniston, Gwyneth Paltrow, Owen Wilson, Jake Gyllenhaal, Nicole Richie, Blake Lively, Edward Norton, Selma Hayek, Kim Cattrall, Colin Farrell, Alicia Silverstone, Russell Simmons, January Jones, Woody Harrelson, Megan Fox, Norma Kamali, Ryan Seacrest, Bethenny Frankel, Jessica Szohr, Elisabeth Hasselbeck, Olivia Wilde, Kim Kardashian, factory workers, supermodels, millionaires, homemakers, and a host of passionate health, diet, and nutrition-concerned consumers. Take a walk in trend-setting Los Angeles or Manhattan, and it appears that almost everyone you see is gripping a bottle or cup of the green stuff. Why are all these people juicing? Because they need energy to keep up with their busy lifestyles, and they have discovered that these nutrient-packed libations supply them with mental clarity, physical energy, and exceptional overall health.

According to recent studies, including some from Johns Hopkins' researchers, only 11 percent of the 24,000 people surveyed eat the bare minimum of two or more servings of fruit and three or more servings of vegetables daily. The USDA recommends 2–4 servings of fruit and 3–5 servings of vegetables daily. The USDA also notes that consumption of these recommended amounts may be low and may not totally meet the daily required nutrients that an individual needs. A study from Dietary Guidelines for Americans says 5–13 servings of combined fruits and vegetables each day are necessary. This is equivalent to about 6½–8 cups, combined, of fruits and vegetables daily.

Canadian studies show that the largest portion of our daily consumption should come from vegetables and fruits. Processed foods do not supply us with the

nutritional benefits of fresh, plant-based foods. Processed foods are low in nutrients and high in calories. The best way to get our daily-required nutrients is from consuming the juice of a variety of raw vegetables and fruits. Just a 16-ounce glass of juice daily will help you reach your recommended daily intake. It would take a lot of chewing, and considerable time, to consume the amount of produce that goes into one 16-ounce glass of juice.

When drinking fresh juices, our cells quickly assimilate the nutrients found in the plants. Eating a raw carrot will give only a small portion of the beta-carotene needed, approximately 3 percent. We absorb even less when we eat a cooked carrot. When juicing that same carrot we get 100 percent of the beta-carotene, because the juice is extracted from the carrot and the nutrients are not trapped in the fiber. As a result, the concentrated nutrients in the juice enter the bloodstream and assimilate quickly. Why is this important? One reason is because drinking juice gives our body's digestive system a needed rest. Our bodies can instead use this energy to help boost our immune system. This is one reason why juice fasting is so good for antiaging.

Should Juicing Become Your New Main Squeeze?

You might still be asking yourself, what is juicing all about? You might have tried juicing or know someone who has, but you've never really understood if juicing was right for you. You might feel you don't have a half hour a day to make a healthy juice. But the simple truth is, you can make the time to juice. Undoubtedly, you know that you need 7–8 hours of sleep a night to regenerate. This leaves you with 15–16 hours every day. How will you spend that time? Work might take up many of those precious hours, as might your family and household responsibilities. But somewhere in those 15–16 hours you can (and actually must) carve out a bit of time for your health. The little amount of time it takes you to juice daily can

add many good years to your life. If you take the time now, then you may not need to spend time later attending frequent doctor visits or hooked up to a machine on a weekly basis.

There are many sound reasons why juicing just might be what you've been looking for to improve your energy, vitality, and overall health. Most every health expert tells us that vegetables and fruits are necessary to maintain a healthy body. Fresh vegetables and fruits hold amazing power to revitalize our health at any age. Health enthusiasts have turned to juicing in order to consume enough fruit and vegetable nutrients. Some critics claim that juicing is a "craze," and other naysayers think that juicing means refined commercial juice, which is processed and loaded with sugars. Still other skeptics say juicing is junk food and maintain that we should only eat whole fruits and vegetables.

These critics might not have seen or heard of the many testimonies from people of all ages around the world who have credited juicing with improving their overall health and well being, reversing diseases, and remedying a host of illnesses. Juicing plant-based foods has allowed millions of people to reach a healthy weight. Juicing has helped people manage and even reverse chronic diseases like type 2 diabetes.

Although success stories are ahead of the available research (there has not been much done that proves juicing to be healthier than eating the whole fruits and vegetables), it is indisputable that juicing helps us to regularly consume high volumes of fruits and vegetables that we might not have the time or interest in eating. Juicing is not about replacing a balanced diet, it's about adding to it.

Raw fruits and vegetables contain more vitamins and minerals than cooked vegetables. Vegetables in their raw state help prevent disease, because they can nourish every cell in the body. Drinking juiced vegetables flushes the system of waste, and by detoxifying the body, juicing can have a considerable positive impact on many illnesses.

Juicing helps the body to absorb all the nutrients the fruit or vegetables have to offer. These highly concentrated vitamins and nutrients, which directly enter our bloodstream and are assimilated quickly, help to keep our bodies healthy. Juice is also hydrating and can assist with weight loss and inflammation.

Dark leafy greens are a major component of juicing and blending. Greens contain essential minerals, vitamins, and amino acids that humans need for optimal health. Some people who are not accustomed to eating greens and are more of the meat and potatoes type might not at first care for the taste of green juices. However, when greens are mixed with sweeter vegetables or fruits, the greens take on whole new qualities because sweeter vegetables and fruits camouflage the flavor of the greens and make the juice tasty. Although green juicing might be an acquired taste, it's worth the trip. And once greens get into your system and you become accustomed to the taste, you will actually start to crave them.

WHAT ARE ENZYMES AND WHY DO WE NEED THEM?

There are thousands of toxins in our environment. Juicing not only helps the body to dispose of these toxins but also provides it with necessary enzymes. To aid in the removal of toxins, organic ingredients are highly recommended. And this is where juicing comes in.

Enzymes may be the key in preventing chronic diseases and extending our lifespan. As we age, we produce fewer enzymes necessary for healthy digestion. Without these enzymes it is impossible for our bodies to properly break down food. One of the main reasons to drink fresh juice is to get the enzymes that come from raw vegetables, leafy greens, and fruits. Just about everyone eats a diet primarily comprised of cooked foods. Enzymes are destroyed or removed when a food is cooked, microwaved, canned, pasteurized, processed, packaged, or genetically engineered. It is 100 percent guaranteed that enzymes are destroyed in any food heated over 115 degrees.

Enzymes are required for every chemical action that takes place in our body. All of our cells, organs, muscles, bones, and tissues function because of enzymes. Everything depends on enzymes, including our immune and digestive system, our bloodstream, spleen, pancreas, kidneys, and liver. No vitamin, mineral, or hormone can do any work without enzymes. Even our ability to feel, think, and breathe are dependent on enzymes. Our ability to utilize vitamins and minerals is run by enzymes. We need enzymes for proper digestion health, antiaging, and cell repair. Undigested food that passes into the colon can cause bloating, cramping, gas, and diarrhea. If you feel bloated or gassy, have rashes, weak nails, thinning hair, dull skin, constipation, diarrhea, insomnia, mood swings, or fatigue, it is likely you are not properly digesting your food.

This need for enzymes is not a new concept. More than 70 years ago, scientists recognized the importance of enzymes contained in raw foods. More recent research has shown that people with chronic diseases or low energy levels may have lower enzyme content in their blood. Some people may think we have naturally occurring enzymes in our body, meaning that we don't need to go out of our way to replace them. It is true we do have naturally occurring enzymes; however, there is scientific proof that indicates our natural enzymes diminish slowly as we age. In practical terms, it can mean we might start noticing little changes such as loss of vitality and stamina, don't recover from injuries as rapidly, or can't seem to digest our food properly and appear to be aging quickly. Many researchers claim the process of aging is nothing more than decreasing levels of enzymes.

Bad dietary and lifestyle habits, including the consumption of sugars, fats, white flour, cooked and processed food; too much stress; and being exposed to environmental pollution might all contribute to enzyme

health benefits of juicing

Helps with chronic illnesses ♥ Strengthens the immune system

Favors anti-aging ♥ Decreases allergies ♥ Increases strength

Promotes better sleep ♥ Aids digestion

Keeps the body hydrated ♥ Removes toxins ♥ Promotes circulation

Boosts immunity ♥ Supports weight loss

Strengthens bones ♥ Helps organs repair

Aids in consumption of required daily amounts of vegetables and fruits

Strengthens hair and nails ♥ Helps remove toxins from the body

Leads to transition into healthier eating habits ♥ Increases mental clarity

Improves emotional balance ♥ Increases energy

Diminishes the need for medication ♥ Decreases depression

Helps reduce or eliminate a plethora of diseases ♥ Makes you feel good all over

Green juices that include dark leafy greens are power-packed with chlorophyll, which oxygenates the body and enables it to release stored toxins.
A green juice will cleanse the lungs, liver, and digestive system. The magnesium in green juices helps to support the utilization of calcium.
What do all plants have in common? Plants are the only type of organism that take light energy from the sun and convert it into sugar. This process, called photosynthesis, allows plants to make their own food and store energy.
All other living things eat plants, or eat things that eat plants, in order to get their energy. It's not a stretch to say that drinking juice is like drinking pure energy!

deficiency. All these factors certainly diminish our health and ability to live a long healthy life.

So, what can we do to increase our enzymes and help our digestion? We can juice raw vegetables, dark leafy greens, and fruits—this will supply our body with needed enzymes. We can promote enzyme activity by consuming fermented foods including sauerkraut, kimchi, and kombucha (see Kombucha recipe page 287). Foods such as ginger, apple cider vinegar, and bitter greens, including arugula and kale, will help stimulate digestion. Chewing each mouthful of salad or raw vegetables 30 or more times, so it mixes with your saliva, will help enzyme activation. If you chew your salad quickly and don't pulverize it in your mouth, you are not getting the full enzyme benefit. The question is how many people chew each mouthful 30–50 times? I would say not many, and this is why fresh organic juicing is a vital addition to our diet.

Of course, not all meals are juiced or eaten raw. But diets consisting of primarily cooked foods leave us enzyme deficient. We must supplement our enzyme reserves in order to fight the degenerative conditions associated with aging. To further aid in digesting cooked foods, supplements such as digestive enzyme capsules might be worth considering. Open up a capsule and sprinkle the contents on the food you are preparing to eat, or take capsules with water before, during, or within thirty minutes after a meal. Enzymes need physical contact with food in order to break down food particles and pass them into the small intestine. Cooked foods will always take longer to digest as compared to raw foods, meaning that cooked foods should be supplemented with enzymes.

Freshly extracted juice is high in enzymes, and they help to both nourish the body and repair cells. We could spend all day chewing in order to consume enough produce to repair or maintain a healthy body. With juicing you only have to drink a glassful to get immediate enzyme benefits. After juicing for a short period of time, you will notice improvements in your digestion.

JUICE PASSION = HOME JUICING

The term liquid lunch takes on a whole new meaning with juicing. In the past, businessmen and women famously had a liquid lunch comprised entirely of alcoholic beverages. But the liquid lunch of today consists of a freshly pressed juice.

You can stop into any of the growing numbers of juice bars or health food stores for a premade take-out juice, which can cost you $10 a bottle. Alternatively, you can have one pressed to order for around $7.95 and upward. Billions of dollars are being spent on detoxifying and cleansing programs that provide anywhere from 1 to 10 days worth of the magic elixir.

Although you might feel these juices do your body good, you may not be able to afford to buy a juice daily, let alone go on a juice detoxifying cleanse for three or more days. This is why so many people are turning to home juicing. Another reason to juice at home is to ensure your juices are organic. Many juice bars use glass bottles, but others use plastic, which may not be the best choice for our health and certainly are not the best choice for the environment. Whatever fresh vegetable juice you decide to consume it is certainly far better than consuming soft drinks. Keep in mind juicing does not exclude eating whole fruits and vegetables. Juicing is just a way to consume more of the important nutrients that add vital vitamins and minerals to our daily diet.

Affordable, newly designed juicers and blenders are easy to use and easy to clean. Once you notice your new glowing skin, newfound vitality, and all the money you save by juicing at home, juicing might very well become a delicious, healthy daily habit. A variety of juicing recipes will help to keep you on track, and that's where *The Ultimate Book of Modern Juicing* comes in.

Easy #10, page 273
Lisa's Gardenx, page 107

THERE'S MORE TO JUICING
THAN MEETS THE EYE

If life hands you lemons, juice them, add purified water, some cayenne pepper, and mint!

If you are new to juicing, I recommend that you find out all you can about the subject. The more you learn about juicing, the sooner you'll be able to discover what works best for you and then incorporate it into your life. This book will give you an abundance of helpful information and enough recipes to keep you satisfied for a good while. The Ultimate Book of Modern Juicing will not only give you many juice recipes but it will also teach you how to use the pulp from juicing to create delicious crackers, breads, and burgers.

Many people are concerned about throwing out wilted fruits and vegetables because they misjudged what they needed for a week's worth of juicing. Here you will find information on how to make a grocery list for juicing, and how to shop and store your produce for a week's juicing. This book is here to help you solve the problem of waste and save you money.

Children are exposed to a plethora of junk food and sugary drinks. Getting children involved in juicing is an important way to start them off on a healthy eating path for life. I'll show you how to teach children to juice, along with how to incorporate more vegetables into their diet. You will also find kid-tested juice recipes.

This book will describe to you how to make Kombucha, which is a fermented tea with exceptional properties to aid in digestion. You will find instructions for how to make a Kombucha starter called a scoby, or mother, which is necessary for the fermenting process. Flavoring techniques, including the use of high antioxidant fruits and healing herbs, are also included.

You'll also find an exploration of just how Mother Nature's vegetables mirror our body parts. For example, the center of a sliced carrot resembles an eye; carrots are known for high beta-carotene, which is good for eyes. Look at the folds in a walnut and it looks like the brain; walnuts contain nutrients that ward off dementia and Alzheimer's. Need a little brain boost? Just toss a handful of walnuts into a blended smoothie recipe. This information and more of nature's wonders can help you bring the appropriate nutrients to your juices. In addition, you will find information on the healing power of herbs and superfoods.

One of the most important and life-saving chapters in this book addresses specific health concerns. The A–Z list of ailments is a good place to start for those people who are working on specific health issues, such as weight loss, diabetes, cancer, depression, acne, allergies, menopause, arthritis, sleep disorders, autism, high blood pressure, cholesterol levels, and much more. This chapter is designed to help you learn what vegetables and fruits to include in your juice recipes, which can help you and your loved ones reverse or prevent many diseases.

Sprinkled throughout the book you will find information on how chemicals, colorants, and additives in our foods and other products affect our overall health and well being.

Juicing Trend

Juicing is growing rapidly in popularity and has become a major lifestyle development among all age groups. Juicing has encouraged many 20- and 30-year-olds to move toward healthier eating. Forty-somethings and baby boomers are seeing and feeling signs of aging and are becoming aware that it's time to improve their health, and adding juices is a good start. Seniors who are seeking ways to reverse diseases and be prescription-free are looking for answers besides drugs and surgery, and so they are giving juicing a try too.

Our social and cultural trends in the United States have opened up new avenues for juice companies who have turned juicing into a $5 billion a year business. But because some juices purchased at a juice bar can set you back as much as $13 for a custom-made drink with added superfoods, more and more people are deciding to juice at home. They have found that a daily habit of juicing doesn't have to be prohibitively expensive.

A 2014 report claimed there were 6,200 juice bars and smoothie shops in the United States, with more opening daily. Even Starbucks sells some healthy juices. Although many major food-processing companies are getting into the juice business, only fresh unprocessed juice will deliver meaningful health benefits. Juice bars with freshly made juices are helping to educate people regarding the benefits of fresh unprocessed juice, but not all juice bars serve organic juices. On page 46, I discuss why organic produce is important when juicing, which I hope will give you more inspiration to juice at home.

Regeneration is possible at any age. Research is proving that we can live a long, healthy life by incorporating more fresh fruits and vegetables into our daily diet.

Mindful health habits can bring abundant knowledge that we can pass down to our loved ones.

History of Juicing

In case you thought juicing just appeared on the scene a few years ago, or you thought the chain store Jamba Juice invented the stuff, here is a little history lesson on juicing.

150 B.C.—Juicing was mentioned in the Dead Sea Scrolls, which dates back to 150 B.C. to 70 A.D. The Essenes, a desert tribe from ancient Israel, mashed figs and pomegranates together with a pestle and mortar. They claimed that this juice promoted physical strength. Throughout time, fruits such as oranges, pomegranates, and lemons, have been easy to find and cultivate. Many cultures pressed and squeezed fruits like these into beverages.

The mid-third millennium B.C. onward—The pomegranate is mentioned in many ancient texts, most notably in Babylonian texts, the Book of Exodus, the Homeric Hymns, and the Quran. The Ancient Greeks call pomegranate juice a "love potion." Island cultures mashed fruits with water to make cooling drinks. In Peru, passion fruits were mashed with water for a cool beverage. And Koreans have used green juice in ceremonial practice for more than two thousand years.

1910s—Because of an overproduction of citrus fruit in California, orange growers used the opportunity to try pasteurization methods to store and ship orange juice to other cities, making orange juice the first mass-produced juice.

1920s—Max Gerson (1881–1959), a German-born American physician, developed the Gerson Therapy, an alternative dietary therapy that he claimed could cure cancer and most chronic degenerative diseases. Gerson Therapy is based on the belief that disease is caused by the accumulation of unspecified toxins. A disease is treated by having the patient consume a predominantly vegetarian diet that includes hourly glasses of organic vegetable juice and various dietary supplements. Gerson Therapy is still in practice today.

1930s—Norman Walker (1886–1985), an English researcher and author, was the biggest advocate of juicing in the 20th century. He influenced almost anyone who is juicing today. Many claim that Walker lived to be 119 years of age, although the Social Security Administration and his grave marker claim that he was ninety-nine when he died (in his sleep). It has been said that he was mentally healthy and active up to the day of his death. He was the inventor of the Norwalk Hydraulic Press Juicer, which many consider to be the best juicer on the market to this day. Walker discovered vegetable juices while recovering from a breakdown in his early years. While staying in a peasant house during his recuperation, he watched a woman in the kitchen peel carrots. He noticed the moistness on the underside of the peel and decided to grind the carrots, thus making his first cup of carrot juice. Juicing helped him recuperate quickly, and shortly thereafter he moved to California to open his first juice bar. Many new juicer machines are for sale today with modern touches, but the Norwalk remains ranked a top-notch juicer, and has undergone few changes over the years.

1940s—Jay Kordich (1923—) has been juicing since the late 1940s. He was diagnosed with bladder cancer fifty years ago, and unhappy about the treatments available, he went to see Max Gerson who had been successful at treating terminally ill patients. Kordich learned from Gerson that with fresh raw juices and a healthy cleansing diet of thirteen 8-ounce glasses of carrot-apple juice a day, he could cure himself. In 1990, Jay became known as the father of juicing. He started his national television career, making appearances with his own brand of juicer. His award-winning infomercials aired for more than 13 years.

Now in his active 90s, Jay is a great example of how the power of fresh juices and raw foods can engender health.

1950s—Ranging in design from centrifugal to masticating, commercial juicers became available for home use.

1960s—Blenders entered the home market.

1968—Ann Wigmore (1909–1994) was a Lithuanian holistic health practitioner, nutritionist, and whole-foods advocate. She cofounded the health resort Hippocrates Health Institute with Viktoras Kulvinskas (who is still active in his work). Wigmore was known as "the mother of living foods" and was an early pioneer in detoxifying with juices and wheatgrass. She believed living foods healed the body, mind, and spirit. She said, "Chlorophyll will be the principle protein for the coming light-bearing age. When freshly made in a drink it contains synthesized sunshine, plus the electric current necessary for the revitalization of the body, and it will open areas of the brain that man yet knows nothing about."

1970s—Jack LaLanne (1914–2011) was an American fitness, exercise, and nutritional expert, and motivational speaker who is sometimes called "the godfather of fitness" and the "first fitness superhero." He invented two juicers and the saying, "That's the power of the juice!"

1975—Dave Otto (1936—), an early pioneer of juicing, believed that juice could heal just about any ailment. He was convinced that opening a juice shop between two gyms would keep him in business, and he was right. Four years later, in 1979, he moved locations to reach out to the general public. Dave's juice store was the first in Los Angeles. In its current location in West Hollywood, Beverly Hills Juice is where one can always see his cultlike customers, including many celebrities, waiting in line to get nutrient-dense, delicious, and addictive juices and smoothies. Dave has always been committed to making juices that are 100 percent organic. This commitment set Dave apart from the other few juice bars in the early days.

Today, at age 78, Dave still goes to the market to pick out his own organic produce. He is very particular how the produce is washed before it gets juiced. Many years ago Dave created his own hydraulic press that is used in his shop today. Not only does he personally juice on a daily basis, but he also works out daily at the gym. He has been a vegan since 1972, and he never visits a doctor's office.

1980s—Welcome to the inception of the juice box. Juice box drinks were primarily made of diluted juices that contained many more artificial ingredients than real fruit juice. The product's popularity grew throughout the years, but so did Americans' obsession with health and natural products. Juice boxes have evolved and some varieties now contain real fruit juice, as well as add-ins such as vitamins. Juice boxes became a lunchbox favorite for children. However, boxed juice is not considered to be a healthy option, as it's processed. Additionally, many brands of boxed juice contain sugar, high-fructose corn syrup, and artificial colors and flavors. New organic boxed juice is on the market today, but again, these are processed and are not considered to be as healthy as fresh juice. A recent study by Consumer Reports found at least 10 percent of boxed apple and grape juices had more arsenic than what the government says is safe for drinking water, and these same juices contain even more levels of lead than arsenic.

1990s—Jamba Juice was conceived. Now boasting approximately 800 stores in 26 states and with a growing number of international stores, Jamba Juice was primarily a smoothie shop when it opened its doors. It now serves a wider variety of foods and has finally added a few fresh-squeezed juices to its menu. Although Jamba Juice claims that their smoothies are healthy meals and snacks—and they have made changes to replace some not-so-healthy options with more healthy ones—the sugar and calorie content in their smoothies is still high.

2000s—The juice revolution arrived. Many brands of juicers became readily available for home use.

2004—Juice bars and smoothie chains opened up at a swift rate in the United States and spread quickly to other countries. Every food or beverage company began thinking about or doing something to get into this juice and health trend.

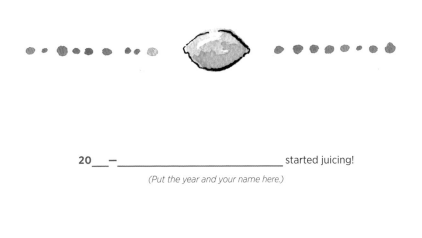

20___–_____ started juicing!

(Put the year and your name here.)

3

JUICING, BLENDING, AND EQUIPMENT

Just because it's green doesn't mean a juice should taste like a newly mowed lawn! Green juices can and should be delicious.

One of the easiest, and in my opinion, best ways to consume high amounts of nutrient-dense, fresh plant-based foods is to extract the liquid from vegetables and fruits with a juicer or blender. Keep reading to learn about the differences between juicing and blending.

Juicing Versus Blending

Which is better, juicing or blending? Some blender advocates say keeping fiber in our juice is important. However, juicing enthusiasts say extracting the fiber promotes better digestion. There is some truth in both of these statements. But this question and debate can be put to rest, because both juicing and blending are important components in any health and wellness program. They both serve a purpose, and both provide a digestible and available supply of dense nutrients.

BLENDING

Blending slows the absorption of nutrients and sugars that enter the bloodstream. Blending is good for people who feel they do not get enough fiber. Blended juices or smoothies can, on occasion, be consumed in place of a meal because the fiber in the blended juice gives the stomach a fuller feeling as compared to juiced drinks. Blending can also be a time saver for people in a hurry because the preparation of vegetables is faster with blending, and with blending there is minimal cleanup. If you enjoy the ease of a blender versus juicer, but you like the qualities of a thinner, smoother juice, then straining a blended drink might be the way to go. A simple kitchen strainer will remove small fibrous pieces from blended drinks. Moreover, not as much produce is used in blended drinks (liquids are typically added to blended drinks in order to create a drinkable consistency). See more in the section Complete Guide to Blending on page 136.

JUICING

Juicing is especially helpful if you have nutritional deficiencies or a weak digestive system. Juicing extracts the fiber from foods, and without the fiber your digestive system doesn't have to work as hard to absorb the nutrients from the drink. Juicing makes the nutrients more readily available to the body. Some people with weaker systems do not tolerate fiber, so juicing could be a good choice for them.

Juicing allows a larger volume of produce to be consumed than blending does because no extra liquid needs to be added. Since a larger quantity of produce is used in juiced drinks, the body is provided with more of the required daily nutrients that it needs. For some people juice is not filling, but for others a juiced drink is filling because of the high volume of vitamins, minerals, and nutrients the body quickly absorbs.

When using a juice extractor (juicer), food pulp is separated from the juice. Pulp is not a throwaway item—it can be used to make raw crackers, breads, veggie patties, and more (see page 296). Pulp also makes great composting material. Older juicers may take a little more time to clean, but newer models are easy to clean.

In the end, it's a personal choice when it comes down to juicing or blending. Some days you might crave a green blended smoothie, and other days you might want the thinner consistency of juice. It's all up to the individual. The point is to get vegetable juice into your body using the method that works best for you. Either way is better than not juicing at all. You can read more in the section Complete Guide to Juicing (page 78)

MOST FREQUENTLY ASKED QUESTIONS

If you have questions about juicing, chances are you'll find the answers here.

Q:

When juicing, where do you get your protein from?

A:

We are conditioned to believe that we need an abundance of protein from animal and dairy sources; however, vegetables such as spinach, kale, romaine lettuce, carrots, turnip greens, collards, broccoli, sprouts, hemp, and chia seeds all contain healthy protein. Many Americans consume twice the amount of protein needed to maintain a healthy body. Excess protein puts a strain on the liver and kidneys because protein can't be stored in the body and is eliminated through those two organs. Excessive protein consumption has been linked to certain cancers, including breast, colon, prostate, and pancreas. Excessive protein can cause kidney disease and osteoporosis. Surprisingly, many people don't know that vegetables contain protein. Drinking a daily juice, or during a juice cleanse, you consume lots of greens and doing so should provide you with enough protein, even if you lead a physically active lifestyle. There are many vegan and vegetarian athletes who build muscle from eating this way and juicing.

Q:

How do I start juicing?

A:

The number one step is to make a commitment to your health. Next, choose a juice from the recipe section in this book that appeals to you. Start with fewer greens and add more as your taste buds get used to them. If you decide to try a juice cleanse for the first time, pick the Easy 3-Day Detoxifying Cleanse Plan (page 262). A few days before starting a juice cleanse, give up meat, dairy, alcohol, smoking, and processed foods. Doing so will help you ease into the cleansing program.

Q:

Do I need to juice every day to get the health benefits?

A:

Our bodies need vitamins and nutrients on a daily basis to maintain good health and keep cells healthy. It is not possible to eat the amount of produce necessary, so juicing daily is the best way to get the required amounts. You will probably not get enough fruits and vegetables in your diet if you are not juicing daily.

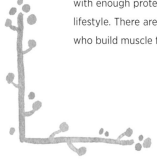

Q:

Can I make enough juice for two days at a time?

A:

Juice oxidizes quickly, decreasing the vitamin and nutrients, so it's best to drink it immediately if possible. Oxidation can slow down when juice is stored properly in an airtight container and refrigerated. It's best to drink juice within 24 hours unless it is made with a cold hydraulic press, which can hold a cold juice fresh for 72 hours and retain its nutrients. If juicing in the evening works best for you, by all means do it that way. Fill your glass container to the very top so no air can get in, then cap with a well-fitting lid to help keep the juice from oxidation. Mason jars work well for storing juice.

Q:

Should I peel my vegetables and fruits?

A:

Nonorganic produce should always be peeled, but there is no need to peel organic produce. All vegetables, including organic, should be toughly washed and scrubbed.

Q:

Do I remove the seeds from apples?

A:

Apple seeds contain small amounts of cyanide. The body can detoxify these in small amounts so many people leave them in. Removing seeds is a personal choice. If you are concerned, core them out.

Q:

When doing a juice cleanse, can I eat something in between juicing if I get hungry?

A:

A juice cleanse typically means you will be only consuming juice. You can also choose a plan that consists of juicing, light salads, and soups, but this type of cleanse will have a different effect on your body than an all-juice cleanse. Consuming only juice without solid foods gives the digestive system a rest, and this is an important aspect of the cleanse. In other words, a cleanse that contains solid foods puts the digestive system back into play. However, if consuming juices, light salads, and soups work best for you, then this is the right cleanse for you. It will certainly make a difference in how you feel, especially if you currently eat a standard diet. However, a juice-only cleanse is advised to achieve a full detoxifying effect.

Q:

How long should I cleanse?

A:

If this is your first cleanse, then anywhere from 1–3 days is recommended. A second round may be extended to 5–7 days. Many people who have extra weight to release or who are trying to get off medications may choose a longer cleanse. As always, check with your doctor or health care provider before you begin.

Q:

Do I need to drink juice on an empty stomach?

A:

Juice should be consumed on an empty stomach. On an empty stomach, vitamins and minerals go straight into your bloodstream. Food can be consumed twenty minutes after a juice. If you eat first, wait about two hours before consuming a juice.

Q:

Which is the best equipment to use: a juicer or blender?

A:

This is a personal choice. When using a blender, the food fiber is still present and the drink has a thicker texture. With a high-powered blender, such as a Vitamix, the fruits and vegetables are blended smoothly, but the drink will still be a thicker smoothie. When doing a cleansing program a juicer is recommended. For daily juicing, both methods work well, and the drinks you make are a matter of personal preference. If you only own a blender but prefer the smoother, thinner consistency of juice, then you can strain the blended liquid. Before making a decision to purchase either a juicer or a blender, if possible try tasting both blended and juiced drinks at a juice bar to determine which might most appeal to you on a daily basis. If you can afford to buy both a juicer and blender, then what you make is a matter of daily preference or need.

Q:

I don't like greens as much as I do fruit; can I use more fruit than greens?

A:

Fruits are high in sugar. They can be used in juicing, but in moderation. Dark leafy greens and a variety of vegetables can be mixed with some fruit, such as apples. However, most juices work best with less fruit and more greens or vegetables. Certainly you can use a little more fruit if you feel your drink is harsh or if you are not used to the green taste. Adding lemon, ginger, or mint will also help to soften the taste. Eventually you will acquire a taste for greens. A good rule to start is 60 percent greens and vegetables, and 40 percent or less fruit.

Q:

I'm on medication for diabetes; should I skip fruit altogether in my juice?

A:

Discuss this with your doctor. Most people with diabetes include one apple or carrot in a juice. Be sure to drink eight glasses of water a day and get plenty of greens in your juices. All fruits contain sugars, and so acquiring a taste for more greens will be helpful.

Q:

Will I lose weight juicing?

A:

Most people lose some weight depending on how much extra weight they are carrying. Some people lose a pound a day when on a cleansing program. The first lost weight is usually water weight. Some people do not want to lose weight and just want to detoxify their bodies. For these people, a short cleanse will be enough. If weight loss is what you are after, eating a plant-based diet along with daily juicing should help speed up the weight-loss process.

Q:

Will my bathroom habits change from drinking juice, and, if so, what should I expect?

A:

Yes, you will find yourself eliminating more frequently. Your urine and stool might change color, but there is no need to be concerned. Your stool could be darker from the greens and the variety of nutrients you are receiving. Beets can change the color of your stool and urine, but don't worry—you are not bleeding to death; a red color is normal when consuming beets. Just keep in mind that juice is a great "house cleaner." Urine should be light in color. Darker urine may mean dehydration, so be sure to drink enough water daily.

Q:

Can I drink warm tea while on a juice cleanse?

A:

Tea is fine, but if you are detoxifying, you don't want any caffeine in your system. If you must drink tea, be sure to drink decaffeinated varieties. And do not drink coffee.

Q:

Can I exercise while on a juice cleanse?

A:

Yes, but not if you have a rigorous schedule, because you might feel the need for some food. A nice walk is usually fine, but while detoxifying it is best to take it easy and relax. Stretching and deep breathing is recommended.

Q:

Will I need supplements and vitamins when I am juicing daily?

A:

You will be getting a large supply of nutrients when juicing daily. It's best to get your blood tested by a doctor to see if you may need vitamin B or D, as those two supplements are what most people are low on. It is advisable not to overload your system with supplements, especially when you are on a cleansing fast. If you take any prescription medications, please consult with your health care provider. Do not stop or reduce your regular medications without your doctor's permission.

Q:

Can I consume the same juice every day?

A:

A mixture of greens is better for you. After all, variety is the juice of life! It's best to rotate the greens in your drink daily. Switching your greens up by using spinach, collards, kale, parsley, chard, dandelion, or romaine lettuce will help prevent oxalic acid build up. Oxalic acid exists in spinach, and this acid is known to affect the thyroid gland and cause some hormone issues. Even so, some raw spinach is a very healthy addition to your diet. Celery, cucumbers, and apples are good choices for daily juicing and make a nice base for other vegetables and fruits.

Q:

How much juice is safe to drink daily?

A:

For an adult who drinks juice on a regular daily basis, or who is detoxifying, three to four 8-ounce glasses daily promotes optimum health. Most juice cleanses consist of six to eight 12- to 16-ounce servings, daily. Remember to drink juice before a meal or between meals, but not with meals. Juice when consumed alone is much more readily digested.

Q:

How long does it take to make a juice?

A:

On average, one juice will take approximately 10 to 15 minutes to make, from the preparation of vegetables to cleaning up. Blender time is shorter. If you are doing a cleansing program, making six 16-ounce juices will take approximately one hour.

Q:

What if I live where I can't purchase leafy greens during winter months?

A:

When greens are not available at your supermarket or farm stand, you may want to add raw organic green powder supplements, including spirulina, blue-green algae, or a combination of green powders to your juice. You can grow sprouts year-round right on your kitchen counter. Sprouts are a good source of protein and are delicious in juices.

Juicers and Blenders

Purchasing a good quality juicer or blender is like investing in a gold mine of health. However, it can get very confusing when trying to decide what equipment to purchase.

Many people assume juicing is a lot of work. No one wants to spend his or her day juicing and cleaning up. Older model juicers and less expensive ones are harder to clean and can become a real chore to maintain. They also don't produce the highest quality juice. The following information will help you in making a choice.

LET'S TALK JUICERS

Throughout history, a variety of juicing tools have been used to separate food pulp from juice. These devices include barrel presses, hand grinders, and inverted cones. Today there are a number of different juicers available for home use. Each separates pulp from juice, but does so in different ways.

HOW MASTICATING JUICE EXTRACTORS WORK

Modern times have produced several kinds of electric juicers, including the masticating type. This type of device is also known as a cold press hydraulic juicer. These juicers have a single-gear motor that slowly kneads and grinds the vegetables. By crushing and then pressing the vegetables, juice is extracted. This type of juicer obtains the highest yield. Masticating/slow juicers are known to produce very little heat, which in turn keeps nutrients intact and oxidation very low. As compared to other juicers, masticating juicers have smaller feed tubes that require more chopping and cutting before juicing. But with a little experience you will learn to do this quickly. Masticating juicers are multifunctional. By using the additional attachments that come with the machine, you can make nut butters, frozen desserts, and baby food. These juicers are easy and quick to clean.

HOW CENTRIFUGAL JUICERS WORK

The centrifugal juice extractor utilizes a fast-spinning metal blade. A mesh filter then separates juice from the flesh of the produce via centrifugal force. The pulp and the juice are separated into different containers. Centrifugal juicers generate heat because of the extremely high speed and lots of friction. Some nutrients, especially live enzymes, can be destroyed by heat. Centrifugal juicers can have a harder time juicing leafy greens and can also leave more pulp in the juice along with a slight bit of foam. Centrifugal juicers take just a little longer to clean than other types of juicers because of the filter screen.

HOW TRITURATING JUICERS WORK

Triturating juicers use twin gears, as opposed to most other juicers that use a single auger. Triturating juicers have two interlocking augers. Vegetables and fruits are not crushed immediately, which allows the ingredients to move slowly as the pulp is separated from the juice. Because of this slower movement, more juice can be extracted from the produce along with high-quality nutrients. Triturating juicers produce more juice than other juicers, which may be beneficial if you juice for the whole family on a daily basis. Like the masticating juicer, triturating juicers are multifunctional. You can use the additional attachments that come with the machine to make nut butters, frozen desserts, and baby food. Triturating juicers have small feed tubes so more cutting and chopping must be done, and because of the slow augers, juicing takes a little more time. Triturating juicers also have more parts to clean and can take a little longer than other juicers for cleanup.

CHOOSING A JUICER

Most inexpensive juicers break down easily and produce low-quality juice. If this is what you have on hand, by all means use it. You have to start somewhere—don't let it stop you. I have not included lower-priced juicers on my juicer list; I have only included those that I know are of superior quality.

I recommend the following juicers for their excellent performance, quality of juice, and easy cleanup. A good-quality juicer will eject the pulp into a receptacle and not keep it in a strainer that needs to be cleaned out

during the juicing process. A high-quality juicer will also have a feed tube and a strong enough motor to help pull the vegetables through without much pushing. A juicer with as few parts as possible makes a faster cleanup. The quality of juice is superior with a good-quality juicer and will retain the most nutrients.

A wide range of juicers can be purchased from my website, YoungOnRawFood.com. There you can read a variety of reviews that may help you make a purchasing decision that fits your budget and personal needs. I have no affiliation with any of these manufacturers and do not receive monetary compensation from them.

EXPENSIVE

The following are expensive top-of-the-line juicers:

Norwalk Juicer—The Norwalk is a hydraulic cold-press juicer that produces 50 to 100% more juice than other juicers. The hydraulic press method of juice extraction also provides a minimum mixing of air with the juices, which results in very slow oxidation or decomposition. This is why many Norwalk juices may be kept refrigerated in closed containers for several days with little apparent loss of flavor, color, or vital elements. This juicer is highly recommended by the Gerson Institute, a nonprofit organization dedicated to the holistic treatment of cancer and other degenerative diseases. The juice from a Norwalk is thin and smooth and very easy to drink. Working with this juicer requires a two-step process. First, you grind the vegetables, and then you scoop the applesauce-like pulp into a cloth that is placed on the hydraulic press shelf. With a switch of a button, the shelf lifts and presses against a stainless steel plate, extracting out the liquid from the pulp (see page 296 for recipes made with pulp). Most juice bars that prepare juice for a cleanse will use a Norwalk because of the shelf life and quality of the juice it produces.

Super Angel All Stainless Steel Twin Gear Juicer 5500—This is another expensive juicer worth mentioning. It incorporates a twin gear impeller press system

that powerfully rotates at a low 86 rpm (the most ideal speed), which keeps enzymes and nutrients alive in the juices. Besides vegetables, a Super Angel Juicer is perfect for juicing wheatgrass, barley grass, leafy greens, herbs, and sprouts. As with the Norwalk, it uses a two stage processing system. The Super Angel is easy to clean and receives great ratings. Highly recommended.

MID-PRICED

The following are good juicers with value pricing:

Kuvings Whole Slow Juicer B6000S—Juicing just became easier with this new vertical low-speed masticating juicer. The feed tube is three inches wide and accommodates whole fruits and vegetables. This feature reduces prep time and maximizes taste and nutrition. This juicer is beautifully designed and comes in silver, white, and red. With a powerful 240-watt low-speed motor that produces minimal vibration and noise, the manufacturer claims that this juicer has the strongest brushless motor in the world. The Kuvings is designed to prevent unwanted oxidation due to cutting, and extracts virtually all of the nutrients in the fruits and vegetables. It comes with a sorbet attachment. Easy to assemble and clean.

Omega J8006—This easy to use, powerful masticating juicer can juice anything from wheatgrass to pomegranates and works at low speeds to yield the most and best-quality juice. Running at 80 rpms, this juicer has a high juice yield and an auto pulp-ejection function for continuous juicing. It has a dual-stage juicing system, is very quiet, and carries a 15-year warranty. The Omega is multifunctional. You can use the additional attachments that come with the machine to make nut butters, frozen desserts, and baby food. These juicers are easy and quick to clean. Highly rated.

Omega VRT350HD or 400HD—This heavy-duty, dual-stage vertical model takes up less counter space than other Omega model juicers. Its low speed juicing prevents oxidation. This model is capable of juicing wheatgrass and gives a superb yield when juicing. It makes nut butters and baby food. Cleanup is easy, and with a 15-year warranty this machine is a good buy. Well rated.

Breville 800JEXL—The Juice Fountain Elite is a 1000-watt juicer with two speed controls. Its sturdy die-cast steel housing and the circular 3-inch feed tube accommodates most whole fruits and vegetables without the need of prep-cutting. It comes with a pulp container, juicing pitcher, and recipe book. It produces a good yield and is easy to clean. Well rated.

Breville BJE820XL—The Juice Fountain Duo Dual Disk Juicer comes with an added purée disk attachment that retains fiber-rich pulp for thick, all-fruit smoothies, sorbets, dips, sauces, and soups. With its heavy-grade die-cast metal body, 1200-watt motor, and 3-inch feed tube that processes whole fruits, this juicer is a good buy. Well rated.

Hurom HU-100—This slow juicer is proven to keep more vitamins and minerals in the juice as compared to high-speed juicers. Energy efficient, this gourmet machine juices vegetables, leafy greens, fruits, wheatgrass, and nuts. It can make nut milks, sauces, marinades, baby food, and ice cream. Well rated.

LOWER-PRICED

These devices can be purchased at most kitchen appliance stores and from online sources. Please read all online reviews before purchasing any equipment. If you don't own a juicer or can't purchase one at this time, you can use a blender and strain the juice through a nut milk filter bag, a paint-thinner bag, or a kitchen strainer.

LET'S TALK BLENDERS

Not all blenders are created equal. A high-powered blender will blend ingredients into a very smooth liquid without any lumps or large particles. Blended juices typically contain some small fiber pieces and feature a thicker consistency as compared to juices from a juicer. The amount of thickness in a blended juice depends on the amount of liquid used.

Straining a blended drink through a nut milk filter bag or paint strainer bag allows you to enjoy a very smooth juice. A smooth juice gives your system a chance to rest during a juice cleanse. Some people enjoy chewing their blended juice and appreciate having the extra fiber. Blended juices and milkshakes are delicious when made in a high-powered blender and can be very satisfying.

When looking for a blender, keep in mind what you plan to use it for. Many blenders are good for making smoothies and have other useful features that allow you to, for example, grind nuts and grains into flour, make soups, nut butters, and baby foods.

EXPENSIVE

Most manufactures of expensive blenders offer refurbished units that are very high quality and come with good warranties. If you are trying to save a little money but still want a high quality blender, refurbished models are a good buy.

Vitamix—This is an exceptional kitchen tool. A Vitamix can be used for many kitchen jobs including making smoothies, milks, sauces, dips, dressings, spreads, soups, flours, frozen desserts, and purées. A Vitamix is made so well it can give you decades of daily use. Vitamix makes several styles. The 5200 model or the Professional Series 750 or Professional Series 500 are all excellent machines. They are easy to clean (self-cleaning), easy to use, and are very durable. Highly rated.

Blendtec—Like Vitamix, Blendtec manufactures high-power, commercial-quality, multifunctional machines. Blendtec offers a wide range of blenders in a variety of prices. Check out the Blendtec Total Blender and Designer Series WildSide Blender Plus. Highly rated.

MID-PRICED

The following are good blenders with value pricing:

KitchenAid—KitchenAid manufactures a variety of blenders. Prices and styles vary, but the KitchenAid Diamond Vortex 5-speed blender KSB1575 gets good ratings. It stirs, chops, purées, and liquefies. In addition to 5 speeds, it also has a crush-ice setting. It comes with a BPA-free pitcher, stainless steel blades, and electronic controls. A powerful vortex adds to its speed, and it blends ingredients together quickly and efficiently. Well rated.

Ninja—Ninja has a variety of blenders. Prices and styles vary, and they are said to be good for the price. I've never tried one, so be sure to read the reviews before purchasing.

LOWER-PRICED

These devices can be purchased at most kitchen appliance stores and from online sources. Please read all online reviews before purchasing any equipment. It's recommended to buy the best equipment you can afford.

Oster Beehive Osterizer Classic 4093—This model includes a two-speed, five-cup glass jar that is dishwasher-safe. Classic and timeless-looking, this 600-watt machine crushes ice, makes frozen drinks, dips, sauces, soups, and blended smoothies. Carries a one-year warranty. Well rated.

Cuisinart—Featuring a variety of blenders with lower-range to premium pricing, some Cuisinart machines double as both blender and food processor. Cuisinart makes very good products and has several blenders that work well for juicing. Well rated.

Hamilton Beach—This manufacturer has a wide range of products in many price points and styles. The 53257 Wavestation Plus Dispensing Blender has a 48-ounce glass jar that is dishwasher safe. The blending action forces the mixture down into the blades, helping to make smooth juices. It crushes ice with its 750 watts of power. Carries a three-year warranty. Well rated.

NutraBullet—If you are looking for a compact machine that breaks down ingredients into a delicious, nutritious, absorptive state then check out the reviews for the Nutra-Bullet. This machine is a great one to take along for traveling. Even if you have other juicers or blenders, this is a good one to own.

Buying Organic

Unlike organic farmers, commercial conventional growers grow a small variety of profitable crops. This strategy is efficient, in that food can be produced cheaply. There are many consequences of this bottom-line mentality for food production. In the past sixty years, for example, there has been a sharp decline in the variety of crops grown in the United States. When crops are not rotated and the same vegetables are planted in the same soil over and over, the spectrum of vitamins and minerals is reduced, and the food produced becomes less nutritious. In addition, conventional growers follow recommendations from the Food and Drug Administration (FDA) regarding which herbicides and pesticides to spray and when to spray them. Although the FDA's job is to protect the public health, rumors persist that the FDA may have financial ties to major food and drug companies and, because of this, make decisions that are more in the interest of these companies than in the interest of the public.

For the last two decades, a trusted resource about these matters has been the Environmental Working Group, (EWG). EWG is an organization that specializes in research and advocacy in the area of toxic chemicals, agricultural subsidies, and corporate accountability. The EWG website provides many consumer guides to a variety of public health issues. See their website, EWG.org.

Using organic produce for juicing is more important than ever before. In fact, organics are important not just for juice, but for all foods. The reason is simple: Commercial farming methods have changed over the years. Commercial crops are routinely sprayed with chemicals, insecticides, and herbicides to control weeds and so-called pests. Recently MSG, Monosodium Glutamate, a flavor enhancer and preservative that can cause many adverse reactions, including headaches, migraines, heart irregularities, seizures, depression, skin rashes, itching, hives, nausea, vomiting, and asthma, has started to be sprayed on food while it is growing to act as a preservative. Moreover, foods are being grown in toxic soils that contain a vast amount of chemicals, pesticides, and petroleum.

More and more, GMO (genetically modified organism) seeds are planted in this contaminated soil, which then leaches into the plant itself. GMO plants are lacking in nutrients and are causing harm to our health. Chemicals in the soil and in the plants that grow in these soils are causing disease and illness in humans. Juicing extracts everything from the plants and fruits, the good and the bad, so it is important to use all, or as much as possible, 100 percent certified organic produce, which excludes GMOs.

One of the guides the EWG publishes is a list called the "dirty dozen." This list contains foods that should definitely be purchased organically grown because these dirty dozen-plus fruits and vegetables hold on to the most chemicals when conventionally grown. The list includes apples, celery, grapes, strawberries, peaches, spinach, sweet bell peppers, imported nectarines, cucumbers, cherry tomatoes, imported snap peas, potatoes, hot peppers, kale/collard greens. To that list we can also add all greens, thin skin fruits, and root vegetables. The EWG also has a list of the clean 15, foods that you do not necessarily need to purchase as organically grown. They include avocado, pineapple, non-GMO corn, cabbage, frozen sweet peas, onions, asparagus, mangoes, non-GMO papaya, kiwi, eggplant, grapefruit, cantaloupe, cauliflower, and sweet potatoes.

Shopping for Produce

Shopping at farmer's markets whenever possible is the best way to purchase foods that are fresh, local, and organic. Foods that are picked ripe and ready-to-eat contain more nutrients than fruits that were picked green and trucked to market. Have you noticed that some fruits rot instead of ripen after you get them home from the supermarket? Or have you noticed many of these supermarket fruits have very little taste? Shopping at farmer's markets and supporting your local organic farmer can ensure that you are getting fresh, local, unsprayed produce that is picked at the proper time. Organic is good for your body and good for the environment.

The Standard American diet (SAD), with its fast foods, refined white flour, highly processed packaged foods, and chemical-laden produce is causing serious health problems for many people, young and old. The late Dr. Linus Pauling, one of the most important scientists of the 20th century and a two-time Nobel Prize winner, said most diseases, illnesses, and ailments in the United States could be attributed to the adoption of commercial farming procedures, which introduced mineral deficiencies in the soil. When food is refined and processed, it loses 90 percent of its vitamin and mineral content.

Certified organic produce is grown in soil that has been declared to be free of prohibited chemical substances for three years prior to harvest. This certification is meant to ensure there is no contamination in the soil, hence the food grown in it. Organic farmers use renewable resources and institute soil and water conservation practices to enhance and sustain the environment for future generations.

Organic foods are important because pesticides have been shown to cause numerous short- and long-term health risks especially in young children, including cancer and birth defects. Some studies claim that organic produce has a higher concentration of vitamins and minerals than conventional produce. Buying organic is beneficial, and the higher cost of organic produce is a small price

#4060 BROCCOL
#4060 BROCCOL
60 BROCCOL
BROCCOL

to pay, even for the budget conscious, when it comes to your health and the health of your family. Juicing organic produce can help you bring your body back into balance.

Bar Codes and What They Mean

Stickers on your food may seem to be annoying at times. But they serve a larger function than just for scanning the price at the checkout counter. The price look-up number, or PLU, on these stickers lets us know how the produce was grown. Using the PLU number, you can quickly and easily determine if a piece of produce was grown with chemical fertilizers, which is known as conventionally grown, if it was grown organically, or if it is genetically modified (GMO).

HOW TO READ BAR CODES AT YOUR SUPERMARKET

Conventionally grown produce, meaning that it was grown with the use of pesticides, has a PLU that consists of only four numbers. Each fruit or vegetable item is given a unique PLU code, which is the last four numbers on the sticker. For example, all bananas are labeled with a PLU code of 4011.

If you find a PLU code with five numbers starting with 8, it means that the fruit or vegetable was genetically modified (GMO). A GMO banana would read 84011.

If you find a PLU code starting with 9, it means that the produce was grown organically and is not a GMO product. An organic banana would read 94011.

PLU NUMBERS TO REMEMBER

5-digits starting with 9xxxx	Organic
5-digits starting with 8xxxx	GMO or GE (genetically engineered)
4-digit starting with 4xxx	Conventionally grown; contains pesticides

At this time in the United States no labeling is required on packaged goods to notify us if GMO food contents are in the package. It is estimated that upward of 70 percent of processed foods on the shelves contain genetically engineered ingredients and can include soups, sodas, crackers, and condiments.

If you don't want to consume GMO foods, you need to avoid nonorganic flax, canola, corn, soy, wheat, USA grown papayas, alfalfa, nonorganic sugar beets, nonorganic milk, cereals, aspartame, and frozen foods. Trace amounts of GMOs can even be in some organic packaged foods. Look for labels that read "Non-GMO Project Verified." For more information visit the website NonGMOproject.org.

There are many developed and developing nations where GMO labeling laws are in place. These countries include 15 nations in the European Union, Australia, Brazil, China, Japan, and Russia. Dozens of countries have banned and restricted importing, distributing, selling, utilizing, and planting GMOs. These countries include Algeria, Brazil, China, Egypt, Germany, Japan, New Zealand, Peru, and the United Kingdom, and also the countries of the European Union.

Not all GMO foods originate in the United States. European countries may use a code from the EAN-13 bar code system. (You may find the meaning of these numbers online.) Additionally, we may not know the organic standards in other countries. Nonetheless, we have a choice to purchase or not to purchase specific foods and products. We do not have to purchase foods that are grown on the other side of the world. We can choose to buy locally in an effort to get the best quality produce, support local farmers, and create less strain on the environment.

NON-FOOD-RELATED BAR CODES

Bar codes are not all necessarily food-related. Some bar codes might instead refer to products that affect food storage containers, kitchen products, and other imported merchandise. As with food, the wise shopper knows where his or her packaging comes from.

The first 2 or 3 digits in a bar code identify a product's country of origin. Nations that commonly supply American markets are noted in the accompanying table.

COUNTRY OF ORIGIN CODES

FIRST DIGITS IN BARCODE	COUNTRY OF ORIGIN
930–939	Australia
740–745	Central America
690–692	China
30–37	France
40–44	Germany
489	Hong Kong
890	India
899	Indonesia
49	Japan
955	Malaysia
480	Philippines
880	South Korea
471	Taiwan
885	Thailand
50	UK
00–09	U.S. and Canada
888	Vietnam

How to Prepare Vegetables and Fruits for Juicing and Blending

Properly washing fruits and vegetables is the best way to avoid food-borne illnesses.

Organic vegetables and fruits do not have to be peeled, but it's advisable to peel sprayed or waxed produce. All fruits and vegetables should be washed and scrubbed even if you are peeling, as bacteria from the outside of the skin can be transferred to the inside when peeled or cut with a knife.

Do not wash produce with soaps or detergents. Soak produce for 10 minutes in 2 tablespoons of distilled vinegar per quart of water. Then soak vegetables for 2 minutes in clean cold water.

Put berries that are fragile including strawberries, raspberries, and blackberries in a strainer and spray with filtered water.

Even when lettuce or spinach is marked prewashed or triple-washed, it's best to rewash again as many of these products are packed in plastic containers or bags.

HOW TO WASH PRODUCE

By following a few essential steps, you can be certain that your produce will be ready for juicing and blending.

1. Wash your hands with soap before cleaning your vegetables.
2. So as not to carry bacteria onto the peeler or knife, wash all produce before peeling or cutting.
3. Carrots and other organic root vegetables often do not need peeling. Scrubbing with a vegetable brush and rinsing under water is all they need. Beets are an exception as the skin is bitter. Peel beets before juicing or blending.
4. Wash all fruit and remove any bruised or damaged parts.
5. Peel back and discard any bruised or limp outermost leaves of lettuce and cabbage.

6. Even if a package says prewashed or three times washed, rewash again as most times the contents have been stored in a plastic container or bag.

HOW TO STORE FRUITS AND VEGETABLES

If possible, it's best to take a few minutes when you get your produce home to prepare them properly for refrigeration. Wrap vegetables in paper towels and store in refrigerator. This will keep them dry and crisp. Place wrapped produce in sealed container or plastic bag. Do not wash produce before storing unless you plan to use it within 2–3 days, as the water will age the produce more quickly. Use what you need daily and rewrap again with dry paper towels.

Fruits may be left out of the refrigerator if you will be using them within a week. Do not refrigerate unripe fruits. Let them ripen on your kitchen counter. Berries stay fresher when stored unwashed in the refrigerator. Lay them loosely in a container lined with paper towels and then cover.

Shop weekly so your vegetables and fruits will be fresh. Do not use old or yellowed greens. Cut bruises off apples before juicing. Bananas that become spotted are ripe and are best for freezing. Peel banana, and break in half or smaller pieces, and then freeze in sealed container or plastic zip top bags. Frozen bananas are great for using in smoothies. Also, you can run them through your juicer for a frozen ice cream treat.

Modern Master, page 97

HEALTH BENEFITS OF SPECIFIC VEGETABLES
FRUITS, HERBS AND SPICES

A green blended smoothie will supply you with 12 or more grams of fiber for a 16-ounce drink.

Experts agree that consuming juice is necessary. With juice or blended drinks made from fruits and vegetables, we can obtain our daily-required supply of nutrients. Find the combinations and consistencies you like best, and try to alternate vegetables and fruits so you get a full range of nutrients. The main thing is to drink fruits and vegetables on a consistent basis.

If any drink leaves you gassy, it could be that you are combining ingredients that do not work well together with your system. It can also mean your body is trying to adjust to some new foods. Try eliminating one ingredient at a time to learn what works best for you. You will learn which combinations are best suited for your digestive system and your body after you have been juicing for a while and your body has gotten used to juicing.

Food Combining

There is controversy among the experts about mixing fruits and vegetables for juicing. The exception is apples, which are said to mix well with everything. Some health advocates say fruits and vegetables digest differently, meaning that mixing them can cause digestive issues like gas and fermentation. Fermentation may occur when food sits undigested in the stomach, which is caused by a lack of stomach acid. Other experts say that when juicing fruits together with vegetables, which include leafy greens, celery, cucumber, and nonstarchy vegetables, the fruits and vegetables get neutralized, balancing the stomach acid. Because juicing separates out the fiber, thus allowing the body to easily assimilate the nutrients in the juice, mixing food types might not be a problem for most people.

Others claim that blending is the best way to combine and consume fruits and vegetables. It has been said that keeping the fruit whole and not separating out the fiber neutralizes the finished drink and aids in digestion. Blender supporters are proponents of chewing their drinks, and in doing so they get a sense of fullness while getting their daily amount of fiber. The Harvard School of Public Health recommends 14 grams of fiber for every 1,000 calories of food, daily. A green blended smoothie will supply you with 12 or more grams of fiber for a 16-ounce drink.

COMBINING VEGETABLES

In most cases, all vegetables can be consumed together, but for optimal digestion it's best not to eat protein and starches together. Protein combines well with nonstarchy vegetables.

Nonstarchy vegetables include beet greens, bok choy, broccoli, brussels sprouts, cabbage, celery, chard, collards, cucumber, dandelion, endive, escarole, fennel, garlic, kale, kohlrabi, lettuce, parsley, radishes, spinach, sprouts, yellow squash, sweet peppers, swill chard, watercress, and zucchini.

Mildly starchy vegetables include beets, carrots, sweet potatoes, and peas.

COMBINING FRUITS

In most cases fruits can be consumed together. One exception is melons, which digest quickly. All melons can be eaten together one hour before or one hour after consuming other foods. In other words, it's best if melons are consumed alone without other vegetables or fruits. Other exceptions might be combining acidic fruits, including oranges, grapefruits, tangerines, or pineapples, with fruits such as dates, raisins, figs, prunes, bananas, papaya, and grapes. These combinations may cause some fermentation and gassing. Fruits, including apricots, apples, blackberries, cherries, grapes, kiwis, mangoes, peaches, plums, and pears can be combined with acidic fruits as well as sweet fruits such as dates, raisin, figs, prunes, bananas, papayas, and grapes.

Health Benefits of Vegetables and Fruits by Color

Western science and Eastern wisdom agree that we should eat foods of every color, as they are disease combating. Eat five-color spectrums every day and you might just live a longer, healthier life.

Green—The green pigment in plants is called chlorophyll. Green foods increase detoxification, circulation, and blood-cell production. Green food contains lutein and zeanithin, which help reduce the risk of macular degeneration and cataracts. Greens contain antioxidants, potassium, vitamin C, vitamin K, and folic acid. Vitamin K can help prevent diabetes and may reduce your risk of pancreatic cancer. There is evidence that suggests eating cruciferous vegetables and dark leafy greens like cauliflower, broccoli, cabbage, and all dark leafy greens help protect against cancer development and growth. Kiwi, avocados,

apples, pumpkin seeds, pistachios, green grapes, limes, and asparagus are all foods you should include in your daily diet.

Orange—Carrots, pumpkins, squash, oranges, sweet potatoes, and orange bell peppers are rich in beta-carotene, vitamin C and A, and can improve eyesight and bolster the immune system. Orange foods have been shown to exhibit anticarcinogenic effects by slowing down and reducing the risk of cancer and heart disease. Eat orange foods at least three times a week.

Red—Tomatoes, red bell peppers, beets, watermelon, pomegranates, and red berries are rich in lycopene, anthocyanins, flavonoids, and antioxidants, which improve heart health and may diminish the risk of ovarian and pancreatic cancer by as much as 60 percent. The pigments in red foods fight free radicals and prevent oxidative damage to cells. Eat at least one serving of red food daily.

Yellow—Lemons, grapefruit, papaya, and yellow bell peppers are rich in vitamin C and flavonoids, which inhibit tumor cell growth and detoxify against harmful substances. Yellow fruits and vegetables contain powerful antioxidants that protect against almost all cancers, especially stomach, throat, mouth, and colon. They also improve eyesight and bolster the immune system. Eat at least one serving daily.

Purple—Rich in antioxidants and phytochemicals, raisins, dried plums, purple grapes, purple cabbage, black mushrooms, eggplant, red berries, blueberries, and blackberries contain antiaging properties and reduce the risk of cancer. Purple foods get their coloring from phytonutrient flavonoids that are known to keep blood vessels healthy, lower risk of heart disease, and can reverse short-term memory loss. Eat one or more servings a day.

White—Garlic, onions, and shallots are rich in phytochemicals and potassium. White foods help reduce cholesterol levels, lower blood pressure, and help in preventing

diabetes and ovarian, colon, and stomach cancers. Allicin, the active compound in garlic, has antimicrobial and antioxidant effects. Allicin is released when garlic is chopped, crushed, juiced, or chewed. Polyphenols found in onions have anticancer effects on colon cancer cells. Mushrooms are high in vitamin D, which may help reduce the risks of ovarian cancer. Add pears, daikon radish, turnips, mushrooms, cauliflower, and pine nuts to your white foods to help lower blood pressure and cholesterol. Eat at least one serving a day.

Health Benefits of Vegetables and Fruits by Name

All vegetables and fruits serve a purpose, as they contain different vitamins and nutrients. Juicing or eating a variety of these foods will help you maintain a healthy body. The produce department in American grocery stores booms with color and energy, whereas the boxed, bagged, canned, and pouched food on supermarket shelves seem to lack any life at all.

Apples are a perfect sweetener as they are low on the glycemic index. They control insulin levels because they release sugars into the bloodstream slowly. Apples are known to reduce intestinal disorders, including diverticulitis and some types of cancers. Apples can aid in detoxifying and removing heavy metals from our bodies such as lead and mercury. They contain vitamins A and C, phosphorus, iron flavonoids, and calcium. The saying "an apple a day keeps the doctor away" might just be true.

Bananas contain vitamin B, which help balance mood swings. They also contain vitamin C, potassium, and magnesium. Bananas are good for smoothies and milkshakes, and can mask the taste of bitter greens. Bananas are high in natural digestible sugar.

Beets contain vitamins A, B, C, and B2. Beets also contain iron, calcium, potassium, and are considered one of the most valuable vegetables to juice for liver and gallbladder detoxification. Beets build up the red corpuscles and stimulate the activity of the lymphatic system throughout the body. Both the root and the leaves are good for juicing. A small amount of beets in juices goes a long way.

Bell peppers of all colors—green, red, yellow, orange, the lesser known chocolate brown, white, and purple—contain a high amount of vitamins C and A. Red peppers have more vitamins and nutrients than the other color peppers because they contain lycopene. The level of carotene, like lycopene, is nine times higher in red peppers than the other colors. Red peppers also have twice the vitamin C content of green and yellow peppers. Both red and green peppers are high in para-coumaric acid, which is known to inhibit the development of stomach cancer. One cup of raw red bell pepper will supply you with 290 percent of the recommended daily allowance of vitamin C and 105 percent of the recommended daily allowance for vitamin A. Count on peppers for vitamin B6. They are also high in antioxidants and fiber. With approximately 30 calories per pepper, this sweet vegetable is great for juicing.

Berries may be little but they are mighty giants loaded with antioxidants that pack a punch! Most fruits and vegetables contain some antioxidants, but berries are high enough in them to help your body fight oxidative stress caused by free radicals. Eating berries can improve your skin and hair, and prevent many diseases. The powerful antioxidants in berries can help prevent memory loss, are anti-inflammatory, aid in joint flexibility, and may be helpful in reducing the risk of cataracts, macular degeneration, and arthritis. Berries can lower cholesterol and blood pressure. Their folate and fiber can aid in weight loss. Strawberries, blueberries, blackberries, and raspberries are powerful superfoods. The antioxidant and phytochemicals in berries may prevent or reverse some effects of aging, including diabetes and some types of cancer. People with diverticulitis and IBS may experience discomfort after eating berries because of the tiny seeds. Conventionally grown berries are sprayed with pesticides to control fungus. Strawberries and blueberries can carry as much as 50 percent pesticide residue, which cannot be washed off. The bottom line is this: you should only eat organic berries.

Broccoli can provide cholesterol-lowering benefits and support the body's detoxification system. Need some vitamin D? Broccoli has an ample supply, along with vitamins C, B9, K, and A, all of which help to keep your metabolism in balance. Don't discard the stems, as they are loaded with nutrients. If the stems are tough, peel them with a potato peeler to remove the outer tough layer. Broccoli plays a vital role in healthy vision and with cellular and immune functions. Just one half cup of raw broccoli contains 20 percent of the recommended daily allowance of vitamin A, which is a beta-carotene.

Cabbage is known as a cruciferous vegetable and could just be one of the healthiest foods on the planet. It's high in sulfur, which purifies the blood. It contains cholesterol-lowering benefits and minerals, including calcium, magnesium, potassium, and phosphorus, and vitamins A, C, E, K, and folate. Savoy cabbage contains sinigrin, which research has paid special attention to as a cancer preventative. Red, napa, savoy, and green cabbage contain antibacterial, antioxidant, and anti-inflammatory properties. Consume cruciferous weekly. Those with hypothyroid should closely monitor their consumption of cabbage.

Cantaloupe is very low in calories. It tastes sweet, is very hydrating, and is full of nutrition, including fiber, beta-carotene, potassium, vitamins C, B complex, A, and folic acid. Cantaloupe is good for the heart, stroke prevention, eyes, and blood. Beta-carotene has been linked to the prevention of cancer. Some studies have shown that cantaloupe can relieve anxiety and calm the nerves. Cantaloupe creates a high juice yield.

Carrots have approximately 52 calories for a one-cup serving. They are a great source of vitamin A, K, and fiber, which are good for skin and antiaging. An article published in the *Journal of Nutrition* claims carrots might protect against ultraviolet rays. Carrots have been shown to reduce the risk of lung, breast, and colon cancer. Carrots can also help prevent infection when used topically. Studies show that high carotenoids, beta-carotene, alpha-carotene, and lutein are effective in lowering the risk of heart disease. Carrots are good for eye health, teeth, gums, and bones. A Harvard University study claims, "People who consume more than six carrots a week are less likely to suffer a stroke than those who consume only a couple carrots a month."

Celery is known for lowering cholesterol levels and high blood pressure. It also contains a high concentration of antioxidants known as flavonoids. One cup of celery juice supplies a total of twelve vitamins and twelve minerals, including vitamins A, C, and K, as well as folate, choline, calcium, magnesium, potassium, and iron.

Cherries can combat post-workout soreness. They are high in antioxidants and melatonin, which aid in bone health, easing arthritis pain, fighting cancer, lowering blood pressure, and reducing inflammation linked to heart disease and diabetes. In addition, they significantly lower blood levels of cholesterol and triglycerides, reduce belly fat, and aid in stroke prevention.

Chard comes in a rainbow assortment of stem colors. Chard has many powerhouse nutritional benefits. It's an excellent source of vitamins K, C, and A, magnesium, iron, potassium, and fiber. One cup of chard is only 35 calories and supplies you with more than 200 percent of the daily requirement for vitamin K. It does contain oxalates, which can interfere with absorption of calcium. As with spinach and other oxalate fruits and vegetables, people with kidney issues need to consume oxalate foods sparingly. Chard has many healthful properties so don't avoid chard. Just rotate greens daily to avoid oxalate buildup.

Cranberries have many medicinal properties that protect the urinary tract from infections and help cure

inflammatory diseases. They are a diuretic, which helps to flush out excess water from the body. Cranberries are a good source of vitamins C and K, and contain minerals including, magnesium, potassium, phosphorous, and calcium. Cranberries can be a powerful antioxidant to stop bacteria in the mouth, which in turn helps prevent cavities and dental plaque. Cranberries contain oxalates, so if you have kidney or gallbladder problems, it is best to use sparingly.

Cucumbers are one of the most economical vegetables to juice; they provide the most liquid for your dollar. A one-cup serving contains 86 to 100 IUs of vitamin A. Vitamin A is a fat-soluble vitamin and antioxidant and is very important for eyesight health. Vitamin A is needed for the health of respiratory, urinary, and gastrointestinal tract. Cucumbers contain calcium, which plays an important part in strong teeth and bones. Cucumber juice helps with digestion, weight control, flushing out toxins, and constipation. The sodium in cucumbers can be helpful with blood pressure regulation and blood vessels. Cucumbers are 95 percent water, which helps to flush toxins from the body. Cucumbers are also good for clearing skin eruptions.

Daikon is a Japanese word that means "large root." This root can sometimes grow to be three feet long and weigh as much as 50 pounds. Daikon is from the radish family. It is white with a smooth skin and a green leafy top and can taste sweet or spicy. The green tops wilt quickly, so most of the time they are removed in the produce department before shelving. When juiced or eaten quickly after cutting, daikon provides an abundant amount of digestive enzymes. Daikon enzymes are comparable to the ones found in the human digestive tract. This root has the ability to increase the absorption of beta-carotene, so daikon is good juiced with carrots, sweet potatoes, and dark leafy greens. Drinking the juice of daikon will help inhibit the formation of chemicals in the body. The juice can also reduce the risk of cancer, as daikon is a cruciferous

vegetable. Daikon juice promotes the release of excess water by the kidneys and can help the respiratory tract and lungs by dissolving mucus. Daikon is high in vitamin C, magnesium, potassium, and fiber.

Fennel is a crunchy, sweet, delicious vegetable. The bulb, stalk, leaves, and seeds are all edible. Fennel is not only good in salads but is delicious in juices. One cup of raw fennel has only 26 calories and can provide you with vitamins C and B3. It contains fiber, potassium, manganese, folate, phosphorus, calcium, magnesium, iron, and copper. Fennel has a very mild licorice taste and is known both as an herb and a spice. It can ease bloating, digestive spasms, and gas pains. Bad breath and body odors that originate in the intestines can be helped with consuming fennel. Fennel might lessen menstrual cramps because its phytochemicals contain phytoestrogen-like compounds.

Grapes contain important minerals, including potassium, calcium, iron, phosphorus, magnesium, and selenium. High in vitamins A, B, C, K, and folate, grapes are a powerful antioxidant that helps the body rid itself from free radicals, making them a good antiaging fruit. Grapes can help keep your immune system strong. Flavonoids found in grapes keep blood flowing freely, helping to prevent clots, strokes, and heart attacks. The potassium in grapes can help lower blood pressure. Because grapes tend to mold and attract insects, growers spray multiple applications of chemicals. Chilean grapes are known to be treated with 17 pesticides. Buy organic.

Grapefruit contains vitamins C, A, B5, B1, and fiber and potassium, and are low in calories. Pink and red grapefruit contain lycopene, a carotenoid phytonutrient. Unlike pink grapefruit, white grapefruits do not contain lycopene. Lycopene foods have the highest capacity to help in fighting oxygen free radicals, which damage cells. As with other foods containing lycopene, grapefruit have been known to help in the risk of developing prostate cancer. Grapefruit juice ranks amongst the highest in antioxidant activity. The phytonutrients in grapefruit spark the enzymes, which help detoxify the body.

Kale is one food you should include in your diet as often as possible. If you break off a piece of kale to taste by itself, you might think it's bitter. But with a little dressing or in juice, it becomes an addictive dark leafy green. Kale has more vitamin C than oranges. Kale is higher than other greens in vitamin A, which is great for vision. This lovely green has more calcium per calorie than milk per serving. Kale is low in calories and high in fiber. This dark leafy green has more iron than beef. The vitamin K in kale protects against various cancers and Alzheimer's disease, and can help lower cholesterol. Loaded with powerful antioxidants, this anti-inflammatory food contains omega-3 fatty acid, fights arthritis, asthma, and autoimmune disorders. These are all good reasons to drink or eat your kale!

Kiwis are beautiful when they are cut open, but their healthful benefits are what really make an impression. This electric fruit with its fuzzy exterior helps your digestion with added enzymes. Kiwi can help manage blood pressure and keep your electrolytes in balance. A unique combination of antioxidants helps protect the cell DNA from oxidative damage, which in turn can help prevent cancer. Vitamin C has been proven to boost the immune system while performing anticlotting benefits. Kiwis detoxify, are low on the glycemic index, and protect from macular degeneration and other eye problems. Kiwi contains high levels of lutein and zeaxanthin, which are both natural chemicals found in the human eye. Kiwi is alkalizing and protects the skin from degeneration.

Lemons are antibacterial, antiviral, and immune-boosting. The health benefits of lemons have been known for centuries. They are loaded with vitamin C, bioflavonoids, pectin, magnesium, and limonene, which promote immunity and fights infections. Lemon juice kills certain types of bacteria that cause acne. Drinking the juice of a half

lemon in warm or room temperature water upon awaking helps to alkalize the body and clear toxins that accumulate overnight in our digestive system. Lemons play a role in immune defense and help with the development of strong teeth, gums, bones, and cartilage.

Limes are good for women's health. Limes contain calcium and folate, which are important for women. Limes are higher in vitamin C than lemons. The pectin content in the pulp is said to be beneficial in lowering cholesterol and is also heart smart. The juice of limes can help prevent formation of kidney stones, as the citric acid breaks down the formation of crystallized calcium. Lime juice in warm water has been proven to help cystitis. Limes have been shown to lower high cholesterol, and the limonoids in the fruit are a detoxifier and antibiotic, which protects against bacterial poisoning.

Mangoes have been around for centuries. Their antioxidant compounds may have many cures. They have been found to protect against many cancers, including breast, prostate, colon, and leukemia. Mangoes are high in vitamin A, which helps to promote good eyesight and prevent night blindness. Although mangoes are sweet they help diabetes by normalizing insulin levels. Their glycemic index is so low it does not spike sugar levels. Mango improves digestion because its enzymes help break down protein. Count on a generous amount of vitamin C, A, and carotenoids in mango to support the immune system.

Melons are rich in potassium, which may help control blood pressure and regulate heartbeat. A potassium-rich diet helps to keep salt from raising blood pressure, and reduces the risk of kidney stones and bone loss. Melons are also abundant in vitamin C, a disease-fighting antioxidant. They are very hydrating and contain beta-carotene, which is capable of preventing heart disease. Melons have been used for weight control because they are low in calories.

Oranges are a favorite. We all know that oranges contain vitamin C, but did you know that oranges help prevent many diseases? Just like lemons, oranges are rich in citrus limonoids and carotenoids. Oranges are proven to help fight various cancers, including lung, skin, stomach, liver, and breast. Orange juice helps prevent kidney disease and the risk of kidney stones. Oranges are full of fiber and can lower cholesterol. Oranges contain vitamins A and C. They also contain potassium, beta-carotene, magnesium, flavonoids, and electrolytes, which help in maintaining a healthy blood pressure, protect the cells and skin from being damaged, and alkalize the body. Polyphenois in oranges help protect against viral infections. Oranges are considered low on the glycemic index, and as long as you don't consume more than one or two at a time oranges will not spike your blood sugar.

Papayas contain papain, an enzyme that helps with digestion. It is rich in antioxidant nutrients, including vitamin C, carotenes, flavonoids, B vitamins, folate, pantothenic acid, potassium, copper, and magnesium. These nutrients promote the cardiovascular system and provide protection for some cancers. Papayas are good for heart health, support the immune system, and have anti-inflammatory effects. Papaya, like most fruits, help prevent age-related macular degeneration. The vitamin C in papaya helps with osteoarthritis and joint health.

Pears, with its many varieties, are one of the highest sources of dietary fiber, vitamins C, K, B2, B3, and B6. Pears contain magnesium, potassium, calcium, and copper. They have anti-inflammatory properties that help protect us from heart disease, type 2 diabetes, and some cancers. Pears can be active in removing acid-binding bile from our body. This easily digested fruit is hypoallergenic, low in acid, and good for lowering the risk of macular degeneration. Pears contain boron, which we need in order to retain calcium, so they have been linked to the prevention of osteoporosis.

Pineapples contain the enzyme bromelain, which is an anti-inflammatory and digestive enzyme. Pineapple helps promote good digestion by helping the body break down proteins. It contains vitamin C and helps keep our immune system healthy. Vitamin C builds collagen, which supports and strengthens our blood vessels, skin, tendons, and ligaments. One cup of pineapple juice contains 11 percent of our daily-recommended allowance of folate and 19 percent of vitamin B6. With just one cup of pineapple juice we get 7 percent of our daily potassium needs. Pineapple is helpful in lowering blood pressure as it contains a generous amount of potassium, which reduces the salt in our system.

Pomegranates have a hard outer shell, but the tiny red inner seeds are worth fighting for. The easy way to open a pomegranate is to place a large bowl or pot in the sink, fill it with water, place the pomegranate in the water, and cut it in half on the round side (not the stem side). Once open, use a finger to break apart the outer shell. Then separate the seeds from the white inner membrane and outer shell. Seeds will fall to the bottom, and the white skin, which is not edible, will float to the top along with the hard outer shell. After the seeds are removed, gently pour off the water. Most of the white skin and shell will follow. Strain the seeds and remaining water, removing any white parts left. Why is it worth the trouble? Pomegranates are a nutrient-dense food source that contains high levels of flavonoids and polyphenois, which are antioxidants. Pomegranates can have higher antioxidants than red wine and berries. Compounds in pomegranates are known to benefit the heart, lower cholesterol and blood pressure, help with heart blockage, and prevent strokes and heart attacks.

Radish roots and leaves are both powerful detoxifiers. Radishes are good for the liver and stomach. Radish purifies the blood and eliminates toxins and reduces the destruction of red blood cells. Radishes are used

for curing inflammation and the burning feeling during urination and help to clean out the kidneys. Very high in potassium, magnesium and vitamins A, B, and C, radishes have a healing effect on the mucus membranes. The flavonoids in radishes can reduce cardiovascular disease and be an anticancer and anti-inflammatory agent. Colon, kidney, oral, intestinal, and stomach cancers have been treated with radishes because of their anticarcinogenic and detoxifying effects. Like all cruciferous vegetables, radishes are packed with antioxidants. Add blood pressure, diabetes, constipation, kidney, liver, gallbladder, and skin disorders to the list of ailments that can be alleviated by the radish. Without doubt, you should give this little root its place in your diet.

Romaine lettuce is one of the top picks for dark leafy greens in juicing because of its sweet mild taste. Not only does this leaf taste good but it is packed full of essential vitamins including A, K, C, B1, B2, and B6, as well as omega-3s, folate, fiber, manganese, potassium, iron, magnesium, calcium phosphorus, and copper. The vitamin C, beta-carotene, folic acid, potassium, and fiber make romaine lettuce heart healthy. These nutrients have been shown to lower high blood pressure.

Spinach is high in fiber, is energy producing, and can boost your brainpower. Although Popeye ate his spinach from a can, it's not suggested you do the same. Raw spinach is a much better choice because it's loaded with phytonutrients, including carotenoids, which provide antioxidant protection for your cells. With only 29 calories per cup, spinach is loaded with a host of vitamins and nutrients. Spinach contains vitamins K, C, A, and E, and iron, calcium, potassium, and phosphorus. One serving of raw spinach provides you with a generous amount of lutein and zeaxanthin, which act as antioxidants and may help prevent cataracts and macular degeneration. Spinach contains oxalate, as do some other greens, fruits, and nuts. Oxalates are naturally occurring substances found in plants and animals. Individuals with kidney stone issues should cut back on oxalate enriched foods. (Cooking vegetables that contain oxalate only reduces a small amount of the oxalate content, although many vitamins and minerals are lost in the cooking process.) Rotating your greens in juicing should alleviate any problems. Those with kidney stones should check with their doctor before eating spinach.

Tomatoes are antioxidant rich and cholesterol controlling, qualities that help fight cancers. Lycopene is a flavonoid antioxidant and helps to protect cells from harmful oxygen-free radicals. Lycopene protects the skin from ultra-violet rays. Another protective compound in the tomato is zeaxanthin, which is known to slow down the effects of age-related macular degeneration. The vitamin A content in tomatoes helps protect mucus membranes and skin, and encourages bone health. Rich in potassium, tomatoes help to control heart rate and blood pressure caused by sodium. Add to that, tomatoes are a source of vital B-complex vitamins, including thiamin, niacin, folate, and riboflavin; and minerals, including iron, manganese, trace elements, and iron. Tomatoes just might be the perfect fruit.

Watercress is a cruciferous vegetable that belongs to the mustard family. It has a slightly peppery taste and is good in savory juices. Watercress contains vitamins A, B1, B2, B6, C, E, and K. Its mineral content includes magnesium, manganese, copper, zinc, and potassium. Watercress also contains antioxidants, carotenes, calcium, fiber, and folic acid. It is known to significantly reduce DNA damage to blood cells, which is an important trigger in the development of cancer. In addition to reducing DNA damage, watercress also increases the ability of those cells to resist further DNA damage caused by free radicals. Watercress is good for skin, hair, nails, eyes, bones, immune system, memory, and blood. When not juicing, watercress is a great tasting green in salads.

Watermelon has a name that says it all. With its high water content, this fruit is very hydrating. When you buy organic, you can juice the rind because it contains important nutrients and vitamins. Watermelon contains lycopene, which is good for heart and bone health. It also contains vitamins A and C, potassium, beta-carotene, amino acid, magnesium, and is low in calories. Flavonoids and carotenoids make this fruit a good choice for antioxidants and anti-inflammatory support. Watermelons contain anticancer agents that can also help reduce the risk of some cancers and strokes. Watermelon seeds are bioavailable, which means nutrients are immediately utilized and absorbed into the bloodstream. These seeds contain protein, iron, and zinc. Seedless watermelons are not always the result of GMOs; they can also be a result of hybridization.

Health Benefits of Herbs and Spices

Any herb or spice may be added to juices or smoothies. Some of these ingredients may be juiced. Others, in powder form, can be stirred into drinks. Learn about these ingredients and try them out. Many herbs and spices can be used to infuse waters. See the recipes on page 290.

Basil is in the mint family, and is rich in antioxidants. Basil can help relieve gas and soothe an upset stomach. Studies reveal that some compounds in basil may be useful in treating arthritis and inflammatory bowel diseases, and it reduces swelling. Basil may also help prevent the effects of aging as it contains properties that kill harmful molecules and prevent damage caused by some free radicals in the liver, brain, and heart.

Cayenne pepper is used in detoxifying programs as it stimulates circulation and neutralizes acidity. Cayenne pepper is used for heartburn, gout, tremors, fever, flatulence, sore throat, hemorrhoids, nausea, tonsillitis, diarrhea, coughs, and upset stomach. Cayenne increases the flow of enzyme production and gastric juices. As a preservative, cayenne is traditionally used to prevent bacteria from contaminating food. Cayenne is used to help treat mild high blood pressure and cholesterol, as it helps prevent platelets from clumping together.

Cinnamon is one of the most healing spices. It is known to enhance blood sugar control in diabetics. Some of the natural compounds in cinnamon can improve insulin functions. Cinnamon is antibacterial and anti-inflammatory. Cinnamon is high in antioxidants, which means it is heart healthy. It can also relieve heartburn and can kill a variety of bacteria-causing illnesses including e. coli and salmonella.

Cloves are known for their anti-inflammatory effects. They also have antioxidant properties, which are known to prevent heart disease and stave off cancer. Cloves can help with damaged bones and arthritis. Cloves have a same component found in cinnamon, which can boost insulin function and help the body use insulin more effectively. Aside from bacteria-fighting powers, cloves are good for toothaches because of its pain deadening antimicrobial properties.

Dill is used to soothe the digestive tract, and treat heartburn and diarrhea. It can also relieve gas and colic, because it breaks up gas bubbles. Dill is rich with chlorophyll, so it is good for sweetening the breath. This herb has high levels of antioxidants and possesses anti-inflammatory properties.

Garlic is antifungal and antibacterial, and may help with sinus infections, yeast infections, and other common diseases. Garlic contains allicin, a compound that decreases cholesterol levels and is known to reduce potential risks of heart disease, blood clots, and elevated blood pressure. Garlic can also reduce the risk of hardening of the arteries, known as atherosclerosis. Garlic contains compounds that can flush out carcinogens, bacteria, and viruses that cause colds and flu. Its high levels of iodine make garlic an effective treatment for hyperthyroid conditions.

(clockwise from top): Hemp seeds, Cacao nibs,
Spirulina, Tumeric, Goji berries, Maca powder,
Chia seeds, (center): ginger, aloe

Ginger is known for alleviating symptoms of gastrointestinal disorders. Ginger possesses antioxidant effects and is an anti-inflammatory. It is effective in preventing motion sickness and is superior to Dramamine. Dizziness, nausea, and vomiting are relieved by consuming ginger tea. Ginger is good for nausea during pregnancy and is completely safe, claims the *American Journal of Obstetrics and Gynecology*. Anti-inflammatory diseases, including osteoarthritis, rheumatoid arthritis, and other arthritis-related problems, respond well when consuming ginger. Pain and swelling are relieved with its regular use. Ginger is anti-inflammatory because it contains free radical protection. Ginger's active components and anti-tumor effects may inhibit the growth of colorectal cancer and may kill ovarian cancer cells. Adding ginger juice to green drinks or making ginger tea can boost your immunity.

Jalapeño peppers contain a rich source of vitamin C, which is an antioxidant that helps prevent damage from free radicals. Jalapeños also contain vitamin A, which supports eye health. They provide pain relief for migraine headaches, sinus headaches, congestion, and can clear mucus from the nose. This spicy pepper is an anti-inflammatory, promotes healthy blood flow, and helps to lower high blood pressure. Studies now claim that the capsaicin contained in jalapeños shows promise for turning off a protein that promotes tumor growth. In an issue of the *American Journal of Cancer Research*, studies show that consuming capsaicin drives prostate cancer cells to kill themselves. Capsaicin is used for weight loss, particularly belly fat, as it increases energy expenditures after its consumption.

Mint is rich in carotenes and vitamin C. It contains essential minerals, including copper, iron, magnesium, potassium, and calcium. Mint is good for heartburn and indigestion. It settles the stomach and relaxes the intestines. Mint is helpful in releasing toxins from the body and helps to clean the liver.

Oregano contains iron, fiber, manganese, vitamin E, and calcium. Oregano is known to treat respiratory tract disorders, menstrual cramps, and urinary tract disorders. It is good for bloating, digestion, and immunity. This herb is high in flavonoids, phytochemicals, and phenolic acid. Oregano can help with headaches and the relaxation of muscles. Make a tea with oregano leaves for an antiviral decongestant.

Parsley has amazing healing properties. It can be much more than mere decoration on a plate of food. This herb has been shown to activate enzymes and neutralize particular types of carcinogens such as cigarette or charcoal grill smoke. The flavonoids in parsley help prevent oxygen-based damage to cells. Parsley contains vitamins C, K, and A, which are all very important in the prevention of many diseases including rheumatoid arthritis, heart disease, and diabetes. Parsley also contains folic acid, one of the most important B vitamins. Folic acid is known as a cancer preventative in the colon and cervix. Other nutrients contained in parsley are magnesium, phosphorus, potassium, calcium, and iron. Parsley is a diuretic herb and can help prevent kidney stones and bladder infections. It also relieves bloating during menstruation. Parsley's high chlorophyll content makes it a good breath freshener.

Rosemary was traditionally used to help alleviate muscle pain, boost the circulatory system, and improve memory. Rich in antioxidants and anti-inflammatory compounds, rosemary can boost the immune system, fight infections, and help ease asthma. Rosemary has been used to help improve digestion and treat indigestion. It may also significantly help in preventing brain aging. A major component of rosemary, carnosic acid, together with its antioxidants, can significantly help in preventing cataracts and promote better eye health. Rosemary is used as an effective hair treatment as it stimulates the hair follicles, and relieves dandruff and dry itchy scalp.

Sage is a natural antiseptic and antibiotic, which helps fight infections. With its estrogenic action, sage is effective in relief of menopausal symptoms, including night sweats and hot flashes. There is evidence that sage may be of value to people with diabetes, as sage may boost insulin action.

Stinging Nettle is a flowering plant. Its leaves and stems are covered with silky hairs, which contain histamine, serotonin, and acetylcholine and can irritate the skin. However, it is a medicinal plant that has been used for hundreds of years to treat painful muscles and joints, eczema, arthritis, gout, and anemia. Many people today use this plant to treat urinary problems during the early stages of an enlarged prostate, for urinary tract infections, for hay fever, or in compresses or creams for treating joint pain, sprains and strains, tendonitis, and insect bites.

Thyme may increase blood flow to the skin, as it contains thymol. Increased blood flow speeds healing. Thyme relaxes respiratory muscles and has been used in treating bronchitis. Thyme may also be a mood lifter.

Turmeric use dates back thousands of years to China and India. It was used for curing ailments, along with other potent herbs. Herbs and spices can add a great deal of health benefits to our diet. Turmeric is on the top of the list with its high antioxidant protection against free radicals. It contains vitamins A, C, and E, which have been shown to prevent cataracts. Turmeric is good for our immune system, eyes, bones, joints, liver, digestive system, cholesterol, circulation, heart health, memory, and blood sugar, to name a few. Turmeric may help prevent or reverse gallbladder disease, Alzheimer's, depression, psoriasis, diabetes, and stroke. Because of its antioxidant properties, turmeric can slow down the aging process. In India, turmeric is considered to be a skin food, and it can be used to make a facial mask. Turmeric's anti-inflammatory effects may help in relieving arthritis and carpal tunnel syndrome.

Superfoods

Superfoods are known to have a high concentration of crucial nutrients, vitamins, and minerals. These nutrient-rich foods are beneficial for health and well being. Superfoods are mostly plant based, with a few exceptions. They can be a powerful source of antioxidants that shields our bodies from cell damage. Superfoods have been proven to help prevent and reverse effects of aging and for playing a role in curing a variety of diseases and illnesses. Some of these superfoods are common and others more exotic. They are all worth knowing about and including in our diet.

Superfoods can be added to any juice, smoothie, or milkshake for an added health boost. Check with your health care provider if you have any health concerns before using them.

Acai is a fruit that contains very high levels of antioxidants, which help fight cancer and heart disease. Pronounced ah-SIGH-ee, acai is native to the rainforest of South America. Acai is one of the few fruits that contain oleic acid—the same good fat found in olive oil. Finding fresh acai is not easy, and you may have an easier time finding it frozen or in powders. Most acai juices on the market usually contain added sugars, so you should stay away from them. Look for powdered or frozen unsweetened acai to blend with your juices and smoothies.

Aloe vera has been used as a healing agent for centuries, including the ancient Egyptians, Greeks, and Native Americans. It's been described as "the plant of immorality." Aloe vera is known to heal many ailments externally and internally, including cancer, ulcers, hemorrhoids, skin disorders and lesions, burns, prostate problems, vaginal irritations, and yeast infections. Aloe vera lubricates joints, the brain, and nervous systems. The span of aloe's healing extends from helping to maintain beautiful skin to helping with irritable bowel syndrome (IBS). Another good reason to add aloe vera to drinks is that it protects the body's immune system and destroys bacteria while slowing down the aging process. Add aloe to your drinks to relieve indigestion, heartburn, acid reflux, and constipation.

Aloe vera can be purchased as a juice, gel, or fresh from the plant itself. It is very easy to grow and is handy to keep near the kitchen in case of burns. The gel is a natural antiseptic and aids in healing. If you use the whole leaf, be careful in handling as the edges are sharp. Cut a leaf off the plant and slice down the center of the leaf to expose the sticky clear substance within. Scrape with a spoon and add to blender. The whole leaf may be juiced. Purchase aloe gel or liquid at your health food store or online, but be sure it is not pasteurized. Look for aloe where only the inner leaf is used, not the whole leaf, and preferably cold-pressed. Aloe vera should be the first ingredient listed on the ingredient list of the product—packaging that proclaims 100 percent pure is not always truthful. An aloe vera extract that is reconstituted will be less potent than in its pure form. Make sure to look for the Certified Seal of Approval that reads "aloe content and purity in this product, International Aloe Science Council (IASC)."

Blackstrap molasses can replenish iron and quickly assimilate carbohydrates. It is a restorative blood tonic for cancer patients and aids in the recovery of side effects from chemotherapy and radiation treatments. Blackstrap molasses can help with fatigue, weight loss, nausea, hair loss, appetite, and depression. Add a small amount to a juice, smoothie, or milkshake.

Blue-green algae is unfortunately named. Although you might think so, blue-green algae is not an algae. Rather, it is a form of plantlike organisms that are a deep, dark green color. It grows in both salt and fresh water, particularly lakes and ponds. Blue-green algae, which includes a type called spirulina, contains valuable nutrients and is high in protein. This chlorophyll superfood contains vitamins A, C, E, B, and B6. It also contains iron, thiamin, folate, and riboflavin. Blue green algae may boost your immune system, and it has antiviral properties. It lowers blood cholesterol levels and reduces blood pressure. It may also improve diabetes, attention deficit hyperactivity disorder, stress, fatigue, anxiety, depression, and premenstrual syndrome.

Cacao nibs are one of the best sources for magnesium, which plays a role in muscle function, circulation, and bone strength. Magnesium must be obtained through food sources, as the body does not produce it. High in antioxidants and easy to assimilate, the health benefits of cacao nibs are many, including boosting energy, elevating mood, and improving cholesterol levels. Cacao nibs are a good way to have your chocolate without added sugar. To obtain the full nutritional value of cacao nibs purchase them raw.

Cacao powder contains flavonoids, which are known to help lower blood pressure and improve blood flow to the heart and brain. Although it contains few calories and is low fat, cacao has a delicious, strong chocolate flavor. To get the full effect of its antioxidant, phytochemical properties, only purchase unprocessed raw cacao powder. Add powders to smoothies and milkshakes. Cacao is not to be mistaken for cocoa or carob.

Chia seeds are native to Mexico and Guatemala, and were an important crop for the Aztecs. Chia seeds can boost energy, lower cholesterol, aid in digestion, support stronger teeth and bones, improve heart health, and stabilize blood sugar. The reason why this tiny superfood can heal so many ailments is because it contains calcium, manganese, phosphorus, omega-3s, and are packed with protein and fiber. Chia seeds are from the mint family. These seeds are known to reduce food cravings and can help you to feel full faster. Because these seeds slow down how fast our bodies convert carbohydrates into simple sugars, researchers believe chia seeds may have benefits for diabetics. When placed in any liquid, chia seeds become gelatinous and swell up like tapioca pearls. Chia seeds may be tasteless, but along with their many health benefits they add a nice texture to juices, kombucha, and infused waters.

Coconut oil is a powerful nutritious food source. Unprocessed virgin organic coconut oil has many health benefits both internally and externally. It is antibacterial, antifungal, antiparasitic, and antiviral. Research links coconut oil to healing infection in the blood and tissues, multiple sclerosis, chronic fatigue, hypoglycemia, gallbladder disease, osteoporosis, Crohn's disease, and food cravings. Coconut oil has high alkaline properties and purifies the blood; it has been shown to improve insulin secretion and utilization of blood glucose.

Flaxseeds are an excellent source of fatty acids, which are essential for human health. Whether golden or brown, they are a great source of vitamins, fiber, and minerals. Flaxseeds contain a compound called phytoestrogenic lignans, which acts like estrogen in the body. Flaxseeds contain linoleic acid and alpha-linoleic acid. They also contain minerals and vitamins including B1 (thiamine), B2 (riboflavin), B3 (niacin), B5 (pantothenic acid), B6, B9 (folate), and C, calcium, iron magnesium, potassium, and zinc. Flaxseeds are a good dietary fiber. Research shows that flaxseeds slow down cancer cell growth. Patients with prostate and breast cancer who had consumed a diet rich in flaxseeds before surgery had lower rates of cancer cell growth in their tumors as compared to patients on other diets. Flaxseeds have been called one of the healthiest foods on the planet. They are known to reduce heart disease, stroke, and diabetes. These claims are made because of the high omega-3 fatty acids, which are key forces against inflammation. Inflammation is the cause of many diseases, including heart problems, diabetes, and arthritis. Flaxseeds contain both soluble and insoluble fiber, which has cholesterol-lowering effects. Flaxseeds can stabilize blood sugar and help intestines to function properly.

Gogi berries are high in antioxidants and rich in vitamin A. Antioxidants minimize damage from free radicals that injure cells. Gogi berries help with mental well being and clarity. They can help you sleep better and are good for calming nerves.

Hemp seeds are one of the most nutritionally complete food sources in the world. These small seeds contain all the essential amino acids and essential fatty acids necessary to maintain a healthy body. With its perfect ratio of omega-6 and omega-3, hemp seeds are a complete protein, rivaled only by spirulina. Three tablespoons of hemp seeds equals approximately 11 grams of protein. Hemp seeds are a great source of protein for vegetarians. These tiny seeds are easily digested and contain 10 essential amino acids. This super seed contains zinc, phosphorus, and gamma-linolenic acid, which is a source of anti-inflammatory hormones that support a healthy metabolism, as well as good skin, hair, and nails. Its antioxidants, vitamin E complex, and trace minerals make hemp seeds an important component in antiaging efforts. Hemp milk can easily be made for use in place of dairy milk, and hemp milk works great in smoothies or for people with nut allergies.

Lucuma is a centuries-old medicinal remedy from South America. It is a satisfying, sweet, and fragrant powder with an abundance of health benefits. Lucuma powder is made from a subtropical fruit. It is gluten-free and contains fiber and antioxidants. Nutrients from lucuma include potassium, calcium, magnesium, protein, and phosphorus. This rich powder is good for teeth, bones, hormone balance, aging skin, inflammation, and tissue regeneration.

Maca powder is made from a root vegetable grown in the Andes. It is dried into a powder. Maca is good for balancing hormones for both women and men. It can boost endurance and supply energy. It's also an adaptogen, which means that it can undo damage from fatigue and helps in regeneration and repair. Maca contains vitamins and minerals including vitamins B, C, and E, amino acids, calcium, iron, magnesium, and zinc. Maca has a nutty, earthy flavor that can be mixed into smoothies and milkshakes.

Mangosteens are grown and highly prized in Southeast Asia for their vast healing properties. Mangosteens have a thick purple rind and a soft interior of white segments. A mangosteen is about the size of a tangerine. The rind contains a compound called xanthones, which is known for combating inflammation and cancer. Mangosteens have been said to provide powerful support for every organ in the human body. They are not easy to find in the United States. Some Asian markets sell mangosteen juice products that contain xanthones from the rind, but the juice may also contain sugars because of the tartness of the rind. When buying the fresh fruit, choose a dark mangosteen with a green top leaf. Mangosteens should have a slight give to the outer shell when ripe and ready to eat. The white segments inside the shell are full of antioxidants. The rind also has many healing properties and can be juiced, but the rind is tart so it's best to add a very small amount in juices that contain other sweet fruits. There is no other description for the taste of the white segments other than to say they are delicious and worth the search.

Probiotics are extremely beneficial for overall good health. They regulate intestinal function and digestion. Probiotics can detoxify the liver and boost energy. They improve immune function, lower cholesterol levels, reduce blood pressure, and improve brain function. Probiotics can also help with irritable bowel syndrome (IBS). You will find probiotics in sauerkraut, kombucha tea, dark cacao, yogurt, and ocean-based plants such as spirulina, chorella, and blue-green algae.

Seaweed or sea vegetables are high in omega-3 fatty acids, which may prevent heart attacks and strokes.

Seaweed is an ancient superfood. It contains minerals such as calcium, potassium, iodine, magnesium, and zinc. Seaweed is high in protein and contains vitamins, A, C, B, fiber, and alpha linoleic acid. It contains antiviral, antibacterial, and anti-inflammatory properties. It also aids in the prevention of degenerative diseases including cardiovascular and diabetes. Seaweed can improve liver function and stabilize blood sugars. It is known to improve memory, lower blood pressure, normalize cholesterol levels, improve the immune system, and help prevent infections. Nori includes almost all the mineral elements that our body requires. The best seaweeds for smoothies are arame, dulse, hijiki, kelp, kombu, and wakame. Powdered kelp and dulse can be purchased for adding to smoothies. Just ½ to 1 teaspoon of powder in smoothies will not overpower the drink. If using dried seaweed, rehydrate by soaking overnight before adding to blender. Seaweeds are salty and have a slight ocean taste, but are delicious when added to green smoothies. Look for certified organic sea vegetables that are tested for heavy metals and residues, including PCBs (polychlorinated biphenyl), fuel oil, pesticides, herbicides, and bacterial contaminants. Untoasted is suggested so as to retain the most nutrients.

Spirulina is a highly bioavailable complete rich protein. It is one of the most nutritious and concentrated food sources on the planet. It is a member of the "blue-green family" but is not an algae. It can lower your cholesterol and blood pressure, and can lessen your chances of developing heart disease, stroke, and cancer. Spirulina contains vitamins B, B12, and K. It also contains calcium, iron, manganese, magnesium, potassium, selenium, and zinc.

Wheatgrass is 70 percent chlorophyll and rejuvenates aging cells, fights tumors, tightens loose skin, and cleanses the blood, organs, and intestinal tract. It is known to reduce blood pressure and remove toxic metals from the body. Wheatgrass is good for all types of cancer, especially of the liver and kidney.

Nutritional Anatomy

Researchers have found that foods that resemble body parts often have health benefits that correspond to that particular body part. When you are at the market, identifying the resemblance of these fruits and vegetables to parts of the body might help you remember what to buy so that you can get a little extra support, for your eyes or your bones or so forth.

BLOOD

Red wine, in moderation, has long been thought of as heart healthy. The antioxidants in wine, known as resveratrol, may help prevent heart disease by increasing levels of high-density lipoprotein (HDL) cholesterol (the "good" cholesterol). It may also protect against artery damage. Red wine resembles blood. A limited amount of wine can aid in blood thinning and reduce blood clots associated with stroke and heart disease. Two small glasses daily are said to aid in longevity.

BONES

Celery and rhubarb have many health benefits. Their long ribs are like the bones in our body and contain vitamin K, which is needed for healthy bones and joints. Interestingly, both celery and bones are 23 percent sodium. When our bodies lack sodium, it pulls sodium from our bones, making them weak. Celery and rhubarb replenish and maintain a healthy bone balance.

BRAIN

Walnuts are housed inside of a shell, and the meat resembles the folds of the neocortex of our brain. Walnuts may reduce or prevent Alzheimer's. Because of their high concentration of omega-3s, walnuts promote healthy brain function.

EAR

Mushrooms, when sliced in half, resemble the shape of the human ear. Mushrooms contain vitamin D, which is known to improve hearing and help strengthen the three small bones in the ear that transmit sound to the brain.

EYES

Carrots when cut in the round resemble the human eye, including the iris and pupil. Carrots protect our vision and help build strong night vision.

FEMALE AND MALE GENITALIA

Figs with their rich history are said to increase sexual powers. When halved, there is a resemblance to female genitalia because of the abundance of seeds. As for looking like male genitalia, figs grow in pairs and are pear-shaped. They are known to increase the numbers and lifespan of sperm and eliminate sterility.

HEART

Grapes hang in clusters and resemble the shape of the heart. Dark grapes have a higher concentration of phytonutrients, which help reduce blood clots, platelet clumping, and heart disease.

Tomatoes also resemble the heart with its four chambers and red color. Tomatoes are rich in lycopene, which is known to help to prevent heart disease.

MALE GENITALIA

Zucchini, bananas, cucumbers are all shaped like male genitalia and are known to have nutrients that strengthen the male sex organ.

MAMMARY GLANDS

Oranges, grapefruits, and other citrus fruits have been compared to the female mammary glands. These citrus fruits contain many nutrients including limonoids, which have been shown to inhibit the development of cancer in the breast.

OVARIES

Olives are a small, oval single-seeded fruit that resemble the ovary. Olives assist the ovary with their rich antioxidant and anti-inflammatory nutrients.

PANCREAS

Sweet potatoes have a shape that resembles the pancreas. Sweet potatoes are beneficial for diabetics as they have a low glycemic index count.

STOMACH

Ginger root looks like our stomach and aids in digestion, nausea, and motion sickness. Ginger has been said to slow down the growth rate of bowel tumors.

UTERUS

Avocados are shaped like a uterus and are a good source of nutrients for reproductive health. Foliate in avocados has been found to reduce the risk of cervical dysplasia.

5

BASIC JUICING RECIPES

For proper digestion, it's best to drink a juice in the morning on an empty stomach, or wait at least an hour or two after eating to consume one.

This section will get you started on your magical juice journey. Here you'll find both helpful information about the juicing process and juice recipes that are healthful for the mind and body.

Complete Guide to Juicing

When using a juicer, also known as a juice extractor, more produce is used to make a 16-ounce juice as compared to a 16-ounce blended juice. For example, when juicing we might use 8 to 10 celery ribs, 3 or 4 large handfuls of dark leafy greens, a few kale leaves, parsley, one large cucumber, two apples, and maybe a few carrots. All this produce would not easily fit into a blender.

Although fiber is certainly good for us, all fiber is not created equal. Cold press juicers and masticating juicers make juice that contains soluble fiber, which allows the body to quickly absorb the maximum benefit from the nutrients, enzymes, minerals, and vitamins that are released from the fiber. Juicing, as opposed to blending, is best for overcoming illnesses because the body does not have to work as hard to digest the juice. For people with weak internal systems, digesting fiber can be more difficult. Juicing is also best for detoxification and healing. Because juice is absorbed quickly into our blood stream, drinking straight fruit juice can spike our blood sugar; however, adding dark leafy greens to juice helps the sugars to neutralize.

Whole or cooked vegetables contain insoluble fibers, which our bodies cannot break down as easily. For an optimum diet, it is advisable to balance both juicing and eating whole plant-based foods.

A glass of juice is considered a meal in itself and is best not consumed with solid foods. After consuming a juice, wait until you are hungry again before eating solid foods. For proper digestion, it's best to drink a juice in the morning on an empty stomach, or wait at least an hour or two after eating to consume one. Drink your juice slowly. This allows your saliva to mix with the juice to promote better assimilation.

Unless you are using a cold-press juicer like a Norwalk, juice is best consumed before nutrients are lost as oxidation begins as soon as the air hits the juice. If possible, drink within 20 minutes after juicing. If you need to juice in the evening because you don't have time in the morning, the best way to prevent oxidization is to pour the juice into an airtight glass container such as a Mason jar. Fill it all the way to the very top so that there is no room for air. When you place the flat cylinder lid on the jar, a little liquid should run over the sides. Then screw the outer rim on. In this way you will be assured that no air is in the jar to cause oxidation. Refrigerate. Once open, drink all the juice.

If refrigerated a second time and the jar is not full, some nutritional content will be lost. But it's still better to have a juice that was refrigerated overnight than none at all.

Many of the following juice recipe combinations can be adapted to a blended smoothie. To make this adaptation, simply use less produce and add filtered water or other liquids of choice.

You may enjoy juicing a recipe and then pouring the liquid into a blender to create an entirely different concoction. Once the juice is in the blender, you can add any number of ingredients that are better blended than juiced. These ingredients include banana, berries, superfoods (see page 70), dates, coconut water, or protein powders. If you are a juicing newbie, this is a good way to sweeten a juice if you need some help adapting to the taste of greens.

THE GOOD NEWS ABOUT JUICING

Juicing, as opposed to blending or eating the whole vegetable and fruit, gives our digestive system a rest while absorbing all the nutrients. Juicing breaks down the food particles before we eat it, which is helpful for people who have sensitive digestive systems or are experiencing special illnesses. Many people who have weak digestive systems should start slowly with juicing. These individuals should begin with a small 8-ounce glass daily and work up to 12–16 ounces as the digestive system starts to improve.

Create Your Own

- Being creative when juicing comes with practice.
- Choose a base that produces a large amount of liquid including any combination of celery, cucumber, and/or carrots.

- Add any hydrating high-water content fruit including apples, peaches, pineapples, grapes, grapefruit, orange, pears, or strawberries.
- Choose one or more dark leafy green.
- Add a little ginger, lemon, or mint if desired to make your own creation.
- If you don't care for the taste you've created, place the liquid in a blender and add a frozen banana. Don't drink juice that doesn't taste good to you, or eventually you will stop juicing. Most juice can be doctored up by adding a little more fruit.

INGREDIENT	APPROXIMATE YIELD
4 medium carrots	½ cup liquid
2–3 celery stalks	½ cup liquid
½ English cucumber or one medium cucumber	½ cup liquid
½ large fennel bulb	½ cup liquid
2 apples	½ cup liquid

Go Bananas

When bananas are speckled with brown spots this means they are ripe and sweet. Peel and freeze them in an airtight container or plastic zip top bags. When the bananas are frozen add them into smoothies and milkshakes. Bananas mask the taste of greens and help children as well as adults adapt to juicing.

Tips for Juicing

- For a quick cleanup, use a recycled plastic bag to line your pulp catcher.
- Juice vegetables or fruits before they are limp or go bad. Remember almost any vegetable or fruit can be juiced.
- If juicing wheatgrass, wrap it in a lettuce leaf as it will juice easier.
- Depending on your juicer, try rejuicing the pulp to see if you get more juice from it.
- Don't let your juicer parts sit too long after juicing or they will be harder to clean. Wash your juicer parts right away or place them in a large bowl of water to soak until you can get to them.
- If storing juice in the refrigerator, always use glass not plastic. Mason jars work well.
- Recipes will say to remove stems from kale leaf, as they are a little strong tasting. Many people enjoy the taste of the stems, so leave them in if you prefer.
- For recipes with a citrus ingredient, either peel citrus and put segments through juicer or juice separately and stir into finished drink.
- Keep in mind that juicing and blending is a healthy daily addition to your diet.

Single Plant-Based Juices

Single plant based juicing is a good elimination diet where you only consume one food or juice at a time, without any solid foods. This can be done during the day with a light meal in the evening, or preferably in a 24-hour period. You can use single plant based juices throughout the day. The following recipes only create a small amount of juice, so if you are drinking throughout the day, you can double or triple these amounts and refrigerate the extra juice until you are ready to drink it. Choose just one of the following for a day of mono juicing. For recipes with citrus, either peel citrus and put segments through juicer or juice separately and stir into finished drink.

- 1 cup pineapple, juiced, and 2 mint sprigs
- 1 cup watermelon, juiced, and 2 mint sprigs
- 1 cup cantaloupe, juiced, and ½ lemon, juiced
- 4 celery stalks, juiced, and pinch of salt
- 1 grapefruit, juiced, and 1 mint sprig
- 2 Granny Smith (green) apples, juiced, and a dash of cinnamon (Note all apple varieties offer health benefits, but some health experts claim green apples are packed with more nutrients and health benefits than red apples.)
- ½ lemon, juiced, or one whole lime, juiced, and 1 cup filtered water

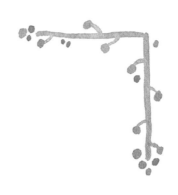

FRESH AND EASY

Cell repair, bone strengthening, and alkalizing. Oranges can lower cholesterol, prevent kidney disease, and reduce the risk of cancer. Add in kale for some vitamin K, antioxidants, anti-inflammatory, and cardiovascular support. Just one stalk of celery can help reduce inflammation, calm the nerves, alkaline the body, and aid digestion. Celery is known to lower blood pressure with its natural sodium content.

INGREDIENTS

1 orange, juiced

½ lemon or lime, juiced

1 apple

3 celery stalks

6 medium kale leaves, stems removed

DIRECTIONS

Use a hand or electric juicer for the orange juice and lemon juice. Set aside. Juice remaining ingredients in order listed, pour into a glass, and stir in citrus juices. (Oranges and lemons can also be peeled and seeded and juiced in the juicer.)

THE BOHEMIAN

Cleansing, calming, and beautifying. There is nothing more hydrating than cucumber to make your skin glow. Along with kale and chard, the superheroes of dark leafy greens, drinking the Bohemian will make your eyes, bones, and teeth healthier. Dark leafy greens are very high in vitamin A, C, iron, and calcium.

INGREDIENTS

1 cucumber

1 apple

3 medium kale leaves, stems removed

3 chard leaves

½ lemon, juiced

DIRECTIONS

Juice all ingredients in the order listed.

EUPHORIA

Cleansing, mood lifting, and cell repairing. Feel a state of intense happiness after drinking this combination of vegetables. Hydrate your skin with a cucumber, push the waste from your body with an apple; and you might be surprised how fennel adds just a hint of sweetness to the taste. Fennel's antifungal and antibacterial properties make it a useful remedy for many common ailments. Fennel is rich in vitamins A and C and many of the B vitamins.

INGREDIENTS

1 cucumber

1 apple

3 romaine lettuce leaves

¼ fennel bulb

6 mint leaves

½ lemon, juiced

1-inch piece of ginger

DIRECTIONS

Juice all ingredients in the order listed.

WAKE ME UP

Purifying, heart strengthening, and potassium building. With just the right amount of dark leafy greens, a carrot to boost your immune system and help your eyesight, and an apple to aid in digestion, this is a juice you will want to wake up for each morning. Add in some turmeric, a powerful anti-inflammatory agent, which helps with a wide variety of conditions including bruises, chest pain, colic, toothache, and menstrual cramps, and you are ready to start your day with a bang.

INGREDIENTS

1 Granny Smith (green) apple

3 carrots

4 kale leaves, stems removed

2 handfuls spinach or romaine lettuce leaves

½ lemon, juiced

2-inch piece of fresh turmeric or a generous pinch of ground

Pinch of cayenne (optional, to taste)

DIRECTIONS

Juice all ingredients in the order listed. If using powdered turmeric instead of fresh, pour juice into glass and stir in turmeric and cayenne.

HOLD ON

Bone building, kidney cleansing, and cholesterol lowering. If you haven't tried juicing red cabbage, you will be surprised at its sweet taste. Red cabbage is loaded with vitamin C, for antioxidant benefits; vitamin A, which promotes eye health; and vitamin K, which protects bones. Add in a handful or two of dark leafy greens for a plethora of nutrition, a carrot for beta-carotene, an apple for lowering cholesterol, a piece of ginger for digestion and you have yourself a bounty of health in just one glass of juice.

INGREDIENTS

1–2 medium pears

1 cup red cabbage

1 apple

1 carrot

2 celery ribs

1–2 handfuls of dark leafy greens of your choice

½ lemon, juiced

1-inch piece of ginger

DIRECTIONS

Juice all ingredients in the order listed.

PERFECTION

Hydrating, blood pressure lowering, and mind enhancing. Apples are known for lowering cholesterol and aiding in digestion. This juice is a winning combination of sweet and greens with a kick of turmeric, which reduces inflammation and is great for your skin. The combination of these ingredients makes up a highly nutritious juice.

INGREDIENTS

1 Granny Smith (green) apple

1 Fuji apple

2 celery stalks

2 carrots

1 medium cucumber

¼ beet with one beet green leaf

1 handful spinach

1-inch piece ginger

Small finger-size piece fresh turmeric,
or powdered if fresh is not available

DIRECTIONS

Juice all ingredients in the order listed. If using powdered turmeric, stir in after juicing.

HOLY MOLEY

Cancer fighting, heart protecting, and immune building. Lots of greens balanced with 1 cup of pineapple, which provides 131 percent of your daily vitamin C, 2 percent of vitamin A, 2 percent of calcium, and 2 percent of iron. Add in cucumber to rehydrate and flush out toxins, and celery, which contains at least eight anticancer compounds, to make this ingredient combination a must in your juicing routine.

INGREDIENTS

1 cup spinach

½ cucumber

4 celery stalks

3 kale leaves, stems removed

1 cup pineapple

8 mint sprigs

½ lemon, juiced

DIRECTIONS

Juice all ingredients in the order listed.

JUST WHAT I NEEDED

Cholesterol lowering, blood sugar regulating, and cardiovascular strengthening. This juice really is just what you needed. Apples inhibit the growth of liver and colon cancers. Green cabbage eliminates harmful toxins and stimulates production of antibodies to fight cancer. Carrots can improve vision, and their high level of beta-carotene acts as an antioxidant to help prevent cell damage, which can slow down the aging of cells.

INGREDIENTS

2 apples

½ cup green cabbage

3 medium carrots

4 chard leaves

½ medium cucumber

DIRECTIONS

Juice all ingredients in the order listed.

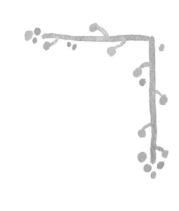

BRAVO LUKE

Kidney cleansing, antioxidant boosting, and heart building. Beets can lower blood pressure, boost stamina, and fight inflammation. Parsley keeps our immune system strong and helps to flush out excess fluid from the body, which supports kidney function. Romaine lettuce has one of the highest nutritional values in the lettuce family. It helps with weight loss, keeps your heart healthy, has a perfect two to one ration of omega-3 to omega-6, and is a complete protein.

INGREDIENTS

½ beet

½ bunch parsley

2 large carrots

5 romaine lettuce leaves

3 celery stalks

1 small piece jalapeño pepper

1 garlic clove or 1-inch piece of ginger

DIRECTIONS

Juice all ingredients in the order listed.

PUMPED UP

Hydrating, blood pressure and cholesterol lowering, and heart protecting. Powerful green veggies and cucumber, which is 95 percent water, are a good reason to have a glass of this juice. Grapefruit is high in vitamin C, which helps to maintain tissue integrity and help our body to produce collagen. Collagen is a structural protein that stabilizes tissues throughout our body. If you take medication, talk to your doctor before consuming grapefruit to avoid a harmful interaction with some medication.

INGREDIENTS

1 medium cucumber

2 celery stalks

2 cups spinach

1 pink grapefruit, juiced

DIRECTIONS

Juice all ingredients in the order listed.

DOWNWARD DOG

Hydrating, detoxifying, and bone building. Need a great pick-me-up after yoga? Try this powerful combination, which will alkalize your body, regenerate your cells, and aid in digestion; and it is a powerful antioxidant and anti-inflammatory.

INGREDIENTS

2 celery stalks

½ cucumber

1 small beet

2 large carrots

1-inch piece ginger

½ lemon, juiced

DIRECTIONS

Juice all ingredients in the order listed.

SUMMERTIME

Hydrating, energizing, and skin repairing. With summertime heat, this cooling drink will quickly hydrate your body and keep you energized for hours. Fennel has high levels of potassium, which is an electrolyte that facilitates brain function. It is rich in vitamin C, which can improve and repair skin tissue, and helps to form collagen. Ice down this summertime juice and put some in your cooler to take to the beach.

INGREDIENTS

1 medium cucumber

½ fennel bulb

2 handfuls spinach

2 celery stalks

2 Granny Smith (green) apples

1 pear

DIRECTIONS

Juice all ingredients in the order listed.

THE GENIUS

Cancer fighting, heart protecting, and blood pressure lowering. You'll know you're smart when you drink this juice; it's packed with superfood greens and just a touch of sweetness. This drink will provide you with a substantial amount of your daily-required vitamins and minerals. You'll notice the added clarity this drink will provide.

INGREDIENTS

1 kale leaf, stem removed

1 handful parsley

1 cup green cabbage

1 cup spinach

2 celery stalks

2 apples

DIRECTIONS

Juice all ingredients in the order listed.

SALT OF THE EARTH

Anti-inflammatory, heart building, and cancer preventing. This juice is a reliable go-to drink. Low in calories and big on vitamin A and C. Romaine lettuce, with its chlorophyll pigment, provides us with powerful antioxidants that are known to help prevent cancer. Add in hydrating cucumber and apple, which contain antioxidants, flavonoids, and phytonutrients, which may help reduce the risk of developing cancer, hypertension, heart disease, and diabetes. You can count on this juice to improve your health.

INGREDIENTS

3 romaine leaves

½ cucumber

1 Granny Smith (green) apple

1 Fuji apple

2 mint sprigs

½ lime, juiced

A pinch of sea salt

DIRECTIONS

Juice all ingredients in the order listed.

THE KICKER

Blood building, cell repairing, and cancer blocking. Beets are sometimes called nature's Viagra. This could be true as beets boost your stamina. They help lower blood pressure, fight inflammation, and help detoxify the body. Add apples, kale, and ginger and you can kick-start your health. Get your daily value of vitamin C with the addition of orange and lemon juice. These two citrus fruits also provide folate, which is critical for the creation and growth of new cells; vitamin B6, which helps regulate sleep and mood; and flavonoids, which prevent the formation of cancers by blocking carcinogenic agents.

INGREDIENTS

½ medium beet

2–3 apples

10 medium kale leaves, stems removed

1-inch piece ginger

1 lemon, juiced

1 orange, juiced

DIRECTIONS

Juice all ingredients in the order listed.

MODERN MASTER

Alkalizing, body balancing, and stimulating. Green is the color of so many things we see in nature. The property of spinach, which is in the same family as beet greens and chard, has many health benefits. In fact spinach is one of the most nutrient-packed dark leafy green: an excellent source of chlorophyll, vitamin A, B complex, C, E, and K. Spinach is highly alkaline and helps regulate the body's pH balance. High in protein, this juice is a must for any healthy diet.

INGREDIENTS

2–3 cups spinach

1 lemon, juiced

1 lime, juiced

Small pinch of cayenne

Stevia or sweetener of choice to taste

1 cup coconut water, stirred in

DIRECTIONS

Juice all ingredients in the order listed.
Stir in coconut water.

SPICE OF LIFE

Mood enhancing, bone building, and cancer fighting. Lift your spirit with dark leafy greens, hydrating celery, cucumbers, and cleansing parsley. Add a touch of daikon, a Japanese name for white radish. Daikon is known for its cancer prevention qualities. It's high in vitamin C, aids in digestion, respiratory health, and is good for the skin, bones, and balancing weight. Just a small piece goes a long way. With added turmeric and ginger you can bet you will feel the spice of life.

INGREDIENTS

3 celery stalks

1 cup spinach

2 Fuji apples

1 medium cucumber

2-inch piece of daikon

1 cup parsley

1-inch piece turmeric

1-inch piece ginger

1 small piece lemon, juiced

DIRECTIONS

Juice all ingredients in the order listed.

GO AWAY

Digestion aiding, blood pressure lowering, and heart healing. Adding citrus to greens gives the juice extra-added vitamin C. Citrus is packed full of good carbohydrates. Dark leafy greens are the superfoods of the plant world and will add the phytonutrients to round out this juice. Garlic has been used for thousands of years all over the world for medicinal purposes. If you are worried about garlic on your breath, take a look at what garlic can do for you and see if it's worth adding to this juice. Garlic is used in treating respiratory problems, poor digestion, bronchitis, fatigue, and parasites. Garlic may help hypertension, tuberculosis, rheumatism, liver disorders, diabetes, high cholesterol, and heart attack and coronary heart diseases. Some people use garlic for the prevention of lung, prostate, stomach, breast, and colon cancers. If you are concerned about the garlic, brush your teeth immediately after drinking.

INGREDIENTS

1 grapefruit, juiced

1 large orange, juiced

2–3 cups spinach

2 stalks celery

1-inch piece ginger

1 garlic clove

DIRECTIONS

Juice all ingredients in the order listed.

RED RULES

Blood building, stamina enhancing, and detoxifying. This juice will help cleanup the liver. If that's not enough, the orange juice adds potassium and vitamin C. Carrots can improve eyesight, regulate blood sugar, promote lung health, and prevent cancer.

INGREDIENTS

½ medium beet

1 large orange, juiced

5 large carrots

DIRECTIONS

Juice all ingredients in the order listed.

GET OUT THE JUNK

Sun repairing, anti-inflammatory, and heavy metal releasing. This drink is very satisfying and comforting. Tomatoes are an important antioxidant that helps protect the damage from sunlight. Lycopene, a red pigment, has demonstrated anticancer effects. Beets (with their detoxifying effects on the liver) and kale contain superior antioxidants. Anti-inflammatory effects are complimented by celery, which is loaded with vitamin A, K, and C. Include some cilantro, which is antibacterial and detoxifies by removing heavy metals like mercury and aluminum from the body.

INGREDIENTS

2 tomatoes

½ medium beet

1 cup cilantro

1 small piece jalapeño (optional)

2 stalks celery

1 lemon, juiced

Pinch of pink Himalayan salt

Purified water if needed

DIRECTIONS

Juice all ingredients in the order listed.

GO GREEN

Alkalizing, deep cleansing, and mood enhancing. Four major dark leafy greens go into this juice, giving it the green light of juicing. These disease-fighting greens are filled with phytochemicals, which help control cholesterol and blood pressure. Leafy greens help temper blood-sugar swings by slowing down the absorption of carbohydrates into your bloodstream after meals. Dark leafy greens can lower your risk of cardiovascular disease and type 2 diabetes.

INGREDIENTS

2 handfuls spinach

6 romaine leaves

2–3 kale leaves, stems removed

4 parsley stems and leaves

1 medium cucumber

5 celery stalks

1–2 Granny Smith (green) apples

DIRECTIONS

Juice all ingredients in the order listed.

BLOODY BRILLIANT

Purifying, blood normalizing, and eye protecting. The health benefits of these five ingredients gives us a great deal of energy and life to our cells. This juice can purify the blood and normalize our blood sugar levels. Beets give us energy by helping our bodies respond better to exercise. Carrots supply us with beta-carotene, which gets absorbed in the intestine and converts into vitamin A during digestion. Cucumber rehydrates us, and the dark leafy greens of romaine lettuce and spinach provide us with chlorophyll.

INGREDIENTS

¼ medium beet

3 carrots

½ medium cucumber

3 romaine leaves

1 handful of spinach

DIRECTIONS

Juice all ingredients in the order listed.

SKIN DEEP

Hydrating, disease defensive, and cell building. Keeping our bodies regulated on a daily basis should be one of our concerns. Apples will help with constipation and cucumbers will give us the added water we need daily to maintain a balanced body. Celery will protect our bones and carrots, our eyes. Basil is an herb in the mint family. Basil can be useful in treating arthritis and inflammatory bowel disease, and is shown to reduce swelling and inflammation. Rich in antioxidants and antiaging properties, basil has been effective in killing off harmful molecules and preventing damage caused by free radicals in the liver, heart, and brain.

INGREDIENTS

1 Granny Smith (green) apple

½ cucumber

2 celery stalks

2 carrots

2 basil leaves

DIRECTIONS

Juice all ingredients in the order listed.

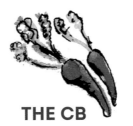

THE CB

Clarifying, soothing, and blood sugar–regulating. This juice will not be forgotten, because of its sweet taste, but there is more to this drink than just sweetness. Carrots, beets, sweet potatoes, apples, and romaine lettuce provide us with a lifetime of health. Mother Nature knew what she was doing when she created such bright colors to dazzle our eyes. Carrots help us to see better, beets help us to think better, sweet potatoes contain iron, which helps us to have adequate energy and a resistance to stress. Apples contain an antioxidant called quercetin, which can reduce cellular death caused by oxidation and the inflammation of neurons. The mighty rich-in-minerals romaine lettuce can help to remove toxins and keep our acid/alkaline balance in order.

INGREDIENTS

2 carrots

½ beet

½ sweet potato

1 Fuji apple

7 romaine leaves

DIRECTIONS

Juice all ingredients in the order listed.

SWEET KARLY

Pain relieving, weight reducing, and bone building. Dark leafy greens have a strong voice in juicing. They are the masters of good health and rich in calcium, which helps keep our teeth and bones strong while reducing the risk for osteoporosis. Romaine lettuce provides us with a healthy digestive track, which in turn gives our skin a youthful glow. Tangerines can help us maintain a perfect weight and will also protect our big generous heart.

INGREDIENTS

7 romaine leaves

3 kale leaves, stems removed

1 cucumber

5 tangerines, juiced

DIRECTIONS

Juice all ingredients in the order listed.

JONAS JUICE

Heart healing, rehydrating, and hangover curing. This juice could not be more perfect. Who wouldn't want to drink this? Just look at what it can do for you. Apples have just the perfect sweetness. Juicing an apple or two a day can help prevent heart disease. Cucumbers are wet and wild and keep us hydrated. We think of carrots as orange, but carrots can be white, yellow, red, or purple. Carrots are one of the most healing foods, providing us with the highest quality in nutrients. Romaine lettuce must be one of nature's best ideas, as it provides us with the sun's chlorophyll. Lemon and mint add just the right touch to put a smile on your face.

INGREDIENTS

2 apples

½ large cucumber

2 large carrots

3 large romaine leaves

1 pear

Handful of mint leaves

½ lemon, juiced

DIRECTIONS

Juice all ingredients in the order listed.

LISA'S GARDEN

Blood sugar balancing, bacteria decreasing, and anticancer benefiting. Growing your own vegetables would be ideal, but not everyone has the time, space, or even a green thumb. Buy these juice ingredients organic whenever possible, then come home and juice a garden in a glass of juice. You might be familiar with the health benefits of the ingredients in this juice recipe, but you might not be familiar with aloe vera. Aloe vera may aid in weight loss, digestion, and immune balancing. You'll want to own your own aloe vera plant once you get to know her. Aloe contains minerals, vitamins, sugars, enzymes, amino acids, fatty acids, salicylic acids, and saponins. What this all means is that aloe covers the bases when it comes to good health.

INGREDIENTS

2 Granny Smith (green) apples

½ piece sweet red pepper

½ large cucumber

2-inch piece aloe vera (see page 71)

1-inch piece fresh ginger

1 small handful leafy greens

DIRECTIONS

Juice all ingredients in the order listed.

THE BIG BANG

Cleansing, digestion aiding, and cancer preventing. How to make a juice stand out? By adding an ingredient you might not have tried before: Kaffir lime leaves. If you are familiar with them, you will know they are used in Southeast Asian cuisine. You might have known they were tasty, but did you know they are also healthy? Thai culture claims this plant to cleanse the mind and body, and can leave you with positive thoughts. They also say it wards off evil spirits. Kaffir lime leaves can help heal teeth and gums, and they aid in digestion and purification of the blood.

INGREDIENTS

1 large cucumber

4 celery stalks

2 medium carrots

8 Kaffir lime leaves

½ lemon, juiced

Pinch of cinnamon

DIRECTIONS

Juice all ingredients in the order listed.

MIA'S CURE ALL

Heart strengthening, immunity building, and weight releasing. Everyone knows tomatoes are good for us, but do you know why? Tomatoes contain vitamin C and are fat free. The list of vitamin content goes on and on. Tomatoes help protect skin against sun damage, and the lycopene in tomatoes makes our skin less sensitive to UV light damage. Tomatoes are good for strengthening bones, so they are a good source to fight osteoporosis. You might notice cucumbers in many of the juices; the reason for that is cucumbers hydrate us both inside and out. We all need as much hydration as we can get. Cucumbers flush out toxins and provide us with heaps of vitamins. Basil, garlic, and lemon are on the list of herbs that cure many ailments. The combination is very powerful, and you will experience a burst of energy after drinking this juice.

INGREDIENTS

1 large cucumber

2 ripe tomatoes

8 large basil leaves

1 clove garlic

Squeeze of lemon juice

Fresh ground black pepper to taste

DIRECTIONS

Juice all ingredients in the order listed.

THE JOZONE

Cancer preventing, bacterial combating, and skin healing. Any lawyer would say there's no argument that this juice is guilty of causing good health. The root of this claim is the daikon radish. Here's the proof. Daikon has shown health benefits for acne, digestive disorders, liver disease, respiratory disease, and sleeping disorders. It's rich in vitamin C and B, and an excellent source of calcium, copper, iron, and potassium. Sweeten the deal with a little pineapple and some dark leafy greens and any jury would find this juice guilty as charged.

INGREDIENTS

3 kale leaves

⅓ cup daikon

1 cup pineapple

4 cilantro leaves and stem

1 lime, juiced

DIRECTIONS

Juice all ingredients in the order listed.

OOH LA LA

Bacteria fighting, antiaging, and anti-inflammatory. This delicious combination can bring you good health. Take lemongrass for instance, which can help rebalance the intestinal flora. Its antiseptic compounds can effectively kill harmful bacteria, yeast, and fungal parasites in the digestive tract, yet it preserves the beneficial bacteria. Turmeric's antioxidant properties may slow down the signs of aging. Its benefits are far-reaching. Ginger improves the assimilation of essential nutrients. It can relieve cramps or indigestion. Its anti-inflammatory effects can bring relief to joint and muscle pain. When sweet potato, spinach, and oranges are added, a balance of vitamin and minerals make this drink indispensable.

INGREDIENTS

1 sweet potato

3 handfuls spinach

3 oranges, juiced

1-inch piece fresh ginger

1-inch piece fresh turmeric

1 lemongrass stalk, white part only

DIRECTIONS

Juice all ingredients in the order listed.

FOUNTAIN OF YOUTH

Age-defying, anti-inflammatory, and cell repairing. As the name implies, this drink may actually just turn back the clock. This drink covers all of the nutrients, vitamins, and minerals we need to keep our bodies healthy. The combination of ingredients adds up to a total balance of health. The bonus is that this drink tastes delicious. Subtract anything you don't like but do give it a try, and you will be quite surprised. This juice makes a good lunch replacement.

INGREDIENTS

2 kale leaves, stems removed

3 ripe tomatoes

½ apple

½ red bell pepper

2 cilantro sprigs

4 basil leaves

½ cup cabbage

1 garlic clove

1 small piece of jalapeño (optional)

½ celery stalk

1 lemon, juiced

DIRECTIONS

Juice all ingredients in the order listed.

LIVING THE DREAM

Heart healing, cancer preventing, and weight managing. Picture yourself lounging on a chair looking at the ocean with a cold juice in one hand and the day ahead all your own. There is something special about this fresh energy-boosting juice combination that can transport you anywhere you want to go.

INGREDIENTS

2 celery stalks

1 apple

⅔ cup mixed berries

¼ beet

2 kale leaves, stems removed

1-inch piece fresh ginger

½ lemon, juiced

½ cup coconut water, added

DIRECTIONS

Juice all ingredients, except coconut water, in the order listed. Add the coconut water after juicing the other ingredients.

TONI'S PARADISE

Detoxifying, bone building, and clarifying. Life is good when you feel healthy. Every ingredient in this juice will add health benefits to your body. Dark leafy greens contain a multitude of our daily requirement of vitamins. Vitamin C is the building block of collagen and supports our bones, skin, and blood vessels. Failing to get enough vitamin C daily can cause inflammation of the gums, skin, and joints.

INGREDIENTS

1 Granny Smith or Fuji apple

1 pear or apple

3 celery stalks

2 kale leaves, stems removed

8 Kaffir lime leaves

1 large orange, juiced

½ lemon, peeled and seeded

Blend in 1 teaspoon maca (see superfoods, page 70), optional

DIRECTIONS

Juice all ingredients in the order listed.

HAPPY HANNAH

Clarity, antiaging, and bone strengthening. Lifting your mood can make a difference in how your day unfolds. There are certain things that can change a dark day into a light one. When you drink alkalizing, stimulating, calming, and cleansing juices like the Happy Hannah, a day can go from dark to light. Adding disease-fighting cranberries can boost your mouth health by stopping acid production. Cranberries can lower your risk of urinary tract infections, prevent certain types of cancers, improve immune function, and lower blood pressure.

INGREDIENTS

2 handfuls spinach

3 romaine leaves

2 celery stalks

½ cucumber

1 cup pineapple

Handful of mint leaves

½ cup cranberries

DIRECTIONS

Juice all ingredients in the order listed.

WALK THE LIME

Anti-inflammatory, detoxifying, and loaded with vitamin C. This juice packs in a whole lot of health. Granny Smith apples lessen your risk of heart disease, diabetes, and stroke. Like limes, Granny Smith apples are high in vitamin C and flavonoids. Cucumbers, which have high water content, help with weight loss. Pineapple is essential for collagen synthesis, and lemongrass is shown to have anticarcinogenic abilities.

INGREDIENTS

1 Granny Smith apple

3 romaine leaves

½ large cucumber

1 pear

½ lime, juiced

1 cup pineapple

2-inch piece of white part of lemongrass stalk

DIRECTIONS

Juice all ingredients in the order listed.

GREEN QUEEN

Builds eye health, lowers blood pressure, and reduces inflammation. This juice combination is a good source of important vitamins and minerals, such as vitamin B6, folate, thiamin, magnesium, manganese, riboflavin, pantothenic acid, potassium, and antioxidants.

INGREDIENTS

3 romaine leaves

2 handfuls spinach

¼ green pepper

Handful of sprouts

1 cup pineapple

1 Granny Smith apple

DIRECTIONS

Juice all ingredients in the order listed.

MAIN KALE

Hydrating, toxin flushing, and blood pressure balancing. Simple but powerful, this juice is infused with nutrient-dense vitamins and minerals. If you don't know enough about kale by now, here are just a couple of its attributes. Kale has zero fats. It's loaded with iron, high in vitamin K, and filled with powerful antioxidants. Pair it with cucumbers (hydrating, antibloating, skin-friendly minerals, and weight loss claims), and you have one healthy juice. Now add in the benefits of grapes, which have the ability to treat fatigue, kidney disorders, and macular degeneration, this juice is even better.

INGREDIENTS

4 kale leaves, stems removed

1 medium cucumber

1 Granny Smith (green) apple

1 cup grapes

DIRECTIONS

Juice all ingredients in the order listed.

PARTY HEARTY

Hydrating, heart healthy, and bone building. Everything in this drink can change the way you look and feel about your health. One glassful and you will immediately feel a surge of energy. Who can resist such power-packed vegetables? This juice can provide much of your daily requirement for vitamins and nutrients. Just in the kale, cucumber, and celery alone you'll get vitamins A, B1, B6, C, D, and K as well as minerals including, folate, calcium, magnesium, potassium, copper, iron, manganese, and phosphorus. Now drink up!

INGREDIENTS

½ cucumber

4 kale leaves, stems removed

1 small handful of parsley

4 celery stalks

3 carrots

2 tomatoes, seeded

DIRECTIONS

Juice all ingredients in the order listed.

TOMATO COCKTAIL

Cardiovascular healing, bone building, and cancer preventing. Most people know a tomato is a fruit, but did you know that tomatoes have high antioxidant properties? Tomatoes also contain lycopene. Studies show that without lypocene in our diets oxidative stress in the bones and unwanted changes in bone tissue occur. Tomatoes contain a host of important minerals. Celery, carrots, and parsley round out this juice to add more vitamins, energy, and life to your day.

INGREDIENTS

4 tomatoes, seeded

3 celery stalks

2 carrots

Small handful parsley

Pinch of chili flakes

Pinch Himalayan salt

DIRECTIONS

Juice all ingredients in the order listed.

ROCKY'S RUN

Anti-inflammatory, hydrating, and bone building. If you're an athlete, you know the importance of vitamins and minerals. Whether you run, ride, or climb, you need to stay healthy. Kale has shown to decrease the risk of oxidative damage to body fats and damage to blood vessel walls. Kale supports the immune system and is abundant in lutein and zeaxanthin, which prevent damage to the eyes from sun exposure. Oranges support heart health, lower cholesterol, and help prevent kidney and liver diseases. Asparagus are loaded with vitamin K for bone strengthening and are high in protein and antioxidants.

INGREDIENTS

3 celery stalks

4 kale leaves, stems removed

2 oranges, juiced

1 handful spinach

3 stalks asparagus, hard stalk removed

½ lemon, juiced

DIRECTIONS

Juice all ingredients in the order listed.

GIDDY UP

Brain building, skin beautifying, and blood sugar regulating. Why drink empty calories and damaging sodas when you can have a delicious-tasting juice that provides plenty of nourishing benefits. An apple a day keeps the doctor away, but this juice has two apples so imagine the benefits. Adding power-packed cabbage to your juice can help prevent headaches, obesity, skin disorders, jaundice, ulcers, cancer, and so much more. Most of us know the power of kale, the superfood of dark leafy greens, and celery to keep our bones strong and our blood pressure down. And with the power of lemon to round off this juice, I think we have a winner here!

INGREDIENTS

2 apples

¼ head of cabbage

2 kale leaves, stems removed

4 stalks celery

½ lemon, juiced

DIRECTIONS

Juice all ingredients in the order listed.

CARROT TOP

Vision improving, cancer preventing, and antiaging. There's more to carrots than meets the eye. Carrots contain a high amount of vitamin A. Deficiencies of vitamin A can cause damage and dryness to the skin, nails, and hair. Vitamin A prevents premature wrinkling and uneven skin tone. Carrots can reduce the risk of heart disease, cleanse the body, prevent strokes, and reduce plaque in the mouth. The carrot's alkaline balances out the acid-forming cavity-forming bacteria.

INGREDIENTS

6 large carrots

1 handful spinach

1-inch piece of ginger

DIRECTIONS

Juice all ingredients in the order listed.

CAN'T BEET THIS

Alkalizing, blood building, and stroke preventing. If you are interested in maintaining beautiful healthy, glowing skin, then this juice is for you. Other benefits that work on the inside as well as the outside are improved vision, reduced risk of cancer and heart disease, flushing the kidneys, building blood, and keeping your mouth bacteria free.

INGREDIENTS

6 large carrots

½ beet

1-inch piece of ginger

DIRECTIONS

Juice all ingredients in the order listed.

THE GUNNER

Poison eliminator, vision improver, and brain booster. Albert Einstein, widely regarded as the greatest scientist of the 20th century, and a lifelong promoter of peace and vegetarian diets, would have certainly loved this juice. Many of the world's greatest thinkers and scientists throughout the ages observed a vegetarian diet from the standpoint of both morality and logic. There's some serious vitamin C, A, and minerals going on in this juice. It will boost your brain power, keep your weight down, calm your nerves, give you a better nights' sleep, alkaline your body, and protect you from many common diseases.

INGREDIENTS

2–3 carrots

½ cucumber

1 handful spinach

2 stalks celery

1 grapefruit, juiced

1 apple

DIRECTIONS

Juice all ingredients in the order listed.

SAVORY JUICE

Brain booster, alkaline balancer, and toxin releaser. Lavish yourself with vitamins A, B, and C, which boost immunity, gives us energy, and keeps us radiant. This potassium-rich drink can keep away many diseases from our body. The folic acid in tomatoes can release the feel-good hormones serotonin, dopamine, and norepinephrine, which regulate mood and sleep.

INGREDIENTS

2 plum tomatoes, seeded

1 small cucumber

½ red bell pepper

2 celery stalks

1 cup parsley

1 lime, juiced

Small piece of jalapeño (optional)

DIRECTIONS

Juice all ingredients in the order listed.

COLD DAY GREEN SOUP

Cholesterol lowering, cancer preventing, and brain boosting. Don't care for broccoli? Juice it and you won't even know it's there. Broccoli is very important in a healthy diet, so you don't want to miss all the benefits. Broccoli has an anticancer compound called sulforaphane, which helps to rid the body of H. pylori, a bacterium found to increase the risk of gastric cancer. Broccoli also contains an anticarcinogen found to hinder the growth of breast, cervical, and prostate cancers. Collards are another vegetable that is not on the "favorite" list, but collards contain vitamin K, which has shown to play a role in increasing bone mass. It also has beneficial effects in Alzheimer's disease by limiting neuronal damage in the brain. With a little spice of jalapeño you will be happy to enjoy this juice soup on a cool or warm day.

INGREDIENTS

2 leaves collard greens

2 celery stalks

1 chard leaf

½ cup broccoli

½ lemon, juiced

1 pear or apple

1 small piece jalapeño or other spice (optional)

DIRECTIONS

Juice all ingredients in the order listed. Warm slightly if desired.

CUCUMBER GAZPACHO

Hydrating, blood pressure lowering, and anti-inflammatory. This drink is rich in vitamin A, C, D, B6, and B1, which are all important vitamins to keep the doctor from our doorstep. Add in folate, calcium, magnesium, and potassium and you have a winning combination to heal and cure a host of common diseases, including high blood pressure and cholesterol, digestive issues, and cancer. Cucumber juice contains a hormone that is used by the cells of the pancreas to produce insulin. Cucumber has been found to be beneficial for diabetic patients.

INGREDIENTS

1 cucumber

3 celery stalks

1 tomato

2 cilantro stems and leaves

½ lime, juiced

Pinch of cayenne or jalapeño

½–¾ avocado

DIRECTIONS

Juice all ingredients in the order listed, except the avocado. Pour juice into blender and add avocado. Blend until smooth.

WARM GREEN JUICE SOUP

Detoxifying, purifying, and repairing. How many of these vegetables would you consume in a day if you weren't making this soup/juice? Let's look at the benefits of some of the ingredients. Broccoli prevents osteoarthritis, reverses diabetes-related heart damage, and reduces the risk of cancer. Kale is a great anti-inflammatory food; it also supports cardiovascular health and provides protein, iron, vitamins, and minerals. Chard, spinach, and zucchini provide a wide range of vitamins, minerals, and omega-3 fatty acids.

INGREDIENTS

½ cup broccoli

2 kale leaves, stems removed

1 chard leaf

1 handful spinach

½ zucchini

½ lime, juiced

1-inch piece ginger

1 teaspoon coconut oil

Pinch of chili flakes

DIRECTIONS

Juice all ingredients in the order listed. Warm slightly if desired. This soup is also very good blended.

Juicing for Children

Not all children like to eat vegetables. Broccoli might just not be your child's favorite, but juicing vegetables with some sweet fruits can be a good way to increase their intake of vegetables and greens. Start them out early.

Five-year-old Kanai loves to get into the kitchen to experiment with food. He uses herbs and spices like a professional chef and loves to make his mom, dad, and sister snacks. The family eats a healthy plant-based diet. They also grow some of their own food. Kanai was happy to help make and test the following recipes in this chapter.

Get children involved with gardening or bring them along to a farmer's market. Let them choose fruits and vegetables they would like to try. When it comes to juice for children or yourself, it is best to choose organic over any chemically treated produce whenever possible.

To prepare produce for juicing, use a vegetable brush to thoroughly scrub the vegetables. Rinse off well before juicing or blending. If you are using inorganic produce, soak, scrub, and rinse well to be sure there are no chemical residues.

Many kids from the ages of two and up whose parents drink juice usually enjoy having a sip or two. Children also enjoy taking part in the process by choosing some of what they want in their drink and dropping it into the blender or feeding it through the juicer tube. You can put the basic greens in and let your child add the fruit. Make it fun, and by adding their favorite fruits, they will soon be asking for more.

Juicing and blending are healthy additions to any child's diet. Depending on the child, you might have to be a little tricky and not let them know you put broccoli or spinach in their juice the first time—but the taste of the fruit will mask what they think they don't like. Eventually they will start to get used to the taste of more greens.

It's no surprise that when children are involved in making a juice, they enjoy the taste of the finished product. You are an example to your children, so when you keep yourself healthy by juicing it's the best way to get your child interested.

The best time to give your child a juice is in the morning or midafternoon. Do not serve juices with a meal as they slow down the absorption of nutrients.

For very young children, it is best to dilute juices with water, and then slowly increase the amount of juice. A small 3- to 5-ounce juice is a good amount. Too much juice can cause diarrhea in a small child. Don't rush the process. See what works best for their systems and adjust accordingly. Children who juice are less likely to get sick. Juicing teaches children about healthy eating habits, which just might ensure a healthier adult life.

Do not substitute fresh juices with the canned, boxed, or jar juices purchased from supermarkets. They are processed and laden with sugars, coloring, and preservatives.

Juice is best served to your child in a cup and not a bottle, as sucking on a bottle keeps the juice on their teeth for a longer period of time and may cause damage to their teeth. Drinking pure water after having a juice will also help wash away any sugar left on their teeth. Or a good brushing is recommended.

Many children prefer a juiced drink rather than a blended one, as it's thinner and easier to drink without the fiber. When making a recipe with banana, juice all the other ingredients, then pour the liquid in a blender and add the banana. Try both methods of juicing or blending to see which your child prefers.

Recipes for Children

Adjust recipes to fit your child's taste, adding filtered water to dilute if desired.

THE POPEYE

A little spinach can go a long way in expanding the taste buds of a young person. Adding a little pineapple with all its nutrients and vitamins will give this drink a sweet taste while reducing the risk of lifestyle health conditions and obesity.

INGREDIENTS

1 handful spinach

½ cup pineapple

1 apple

DIRECTIONS

Juice or blend all ingredients, adding water when needed if blending.

THE SUPERHERO

We all know by now that dark leafy greens are said to promote strong bones and are loaded with almost all the daily-needed vitamins and minerals. Apples contain vitamin A, C, flavonoids, and calcium—all good for growing children.

INGREDIENTS

3 romaine lettuce leaves

1 kale leaf, stem removed

1 stalk celery

1 Fuji apple

Squeeze of lemon

DIRECTIONS

Juice or blend all ingredients, adding water as needed if blending.

THE RED ROOSTER

Iron, calcium, and potassium are all good for growing children. It just might be easier to get children to drink their veggies than trying to get them to eat them, especially if it tastes as good as this one.

INGREDIENTS

¼ beet

1 red apple

1 handful strawberries

½ cucumber

1 small handful spinach

DIRECTIONS

Juice or blend all ingredients, adding water as needed if blending.

DINOSAURS

The perfect combination of fruits and greens ensure you are giving your child a balanced diet filled with vitamins and minerals.

INGREDIENTS

2 kale leaves, stems removed

½ mango

½ cup pineapple

DIRECTIONS

Juice or blend all ingredients, adding water as needed if blending.

JUICEALICIOUS

Just a small amount of juice is enough to nourish your child. Many children eat a bland nutrient-free diet of rice, pasta, and pizzas. Where will they ever get the vitamins and minerals they need for a growing body and strong teeth? Juicealicious can provide a good range of these needed nutrients.

INGREDIENTS

1 Golden Delicious apple

1 handful spinach

2-inch piece of cucumber

1 very small piece of beet

Handful of berries

DIRECTIONS

Juice or blend all ingredients, adding water as needed if blending.

ORANGE FACE

You can find lots of health-building nutrients in this delicious drink, which is a good starter drink to introduce your child to juicing. Be sure they brush their teeth afterward to remove any sugars.

INGREDIENTS

1 carrot

1 orange, juiced

½ Fuji apple

¼ banana

¼–½ cups ice

DIRECTIONS

Place all ingredients in blender, adding water as needed, and blend until smooth.

THE PINEAPPLE TRAIN

Antioxidants and vitamin C are good for us at any age. Muscle soreness, bruising, and strains can slow a child down, but the bromelain found in pineapple can offer many health benefits and quicker healing. Broccoli can be hidden in this juice with the sweet taste of pineapple taking command.

INGREDIENTS

½ cup pineapple

½ apple

1 small piece of broccoli

1 small piece of cucumber

½ celery stalk

DIRECTIONS

Blend all ingredients, adding water as needed.

THE HAPPY BERRY

Antioxidants are important for health at any age, and this delicious drink provides them plus proteins, potassium, and a total of 12 vitamins and 12 minerals.

INGREDIENTS

½ cup berries

½ apple

1 celery stalk

Small piece of cucumber

½ frozen or fresh banana

DIRECTIONS

Blend all ingredients, adding water as needed.

6

BLENDED SMOOTHIE RECIPES

Some days you can enjoy a juice, and on other days you can have a blended smoothie.

The truth is you don't have to be an all-or-nothing enthusiast of either blending or juicing. Some days you can enjoy a juice, and on other days you can have a blended smoothie. You can also have them both on the same day, in the same meal, by combining juiced vegetables and leafy greens from a juice extractor and then pouring the liquid into a blender. To make this into a smoothie, simply add fresh or frozen berries, banana, or other fruits, and blend together. Superfoods including spirulina, gogi berries, maca, oriental herbs or tonics, and protein powders may also be added. This combination method is certainly one to consider.

Complete Guide to Blending

All blenders are not created equal. A high-powered blender like the Vitamix or Blendtec will make your smoothie creamier, which you may find to be more enjoyable to drink. When making a smoothie it is best to use a three-step process. First, add the liquid to the blender pitcher. Second, add the greens and blend well. Third, add remaining ingredients and blend again until smooth. Add more liquid if needed to make your smoothie a drinkable consistency. Gogi berries, maca, green powder, and other superfoods are a good way to give your smoothie a boost. Add superfoods near the end of the blending process.

Green tea is a good liquid to use for smoothies, as are nut or seed milks, coconut water, or purified/filtered water. Green tea can be made the standard way and refrigerated in a Mason jar so that it is ready to use in a morning smoothie. Rather than just using filtered water, using green tea instead will add many powerful medicinal herbs to your blended drinks. Green tea is low in caffeine, less than coffee, (or you can purchase decaffeinated) and contains antioxidants, minerals, and vitamins that will help restore and energize your body. Green tea is also high in the amino acid L-theanine. This has a calming effect and aides with concentration. People will have a different level of alertness when drinking green tea, which many mistake for the caffeine's effect, when it is really the effect of L-theanine. It's high in antioxidants and the benefits are amazing. It also depends on the green tea you purchase. Loose tea has less caffeine than bags, and some green teas are less caffeinated, best to drink in the morning hours. Yerba mate is another powerful antioxidant tea, and it has a higher concentration of chlorogenic acid than does green tea. Chlorogenic acid is known to combat inflammation, reduce cancer cells, clear arteries, destroy bacteria, lower cholesterol and blood pressure, and help with diabetes. Yerba mate also contains caffeine. Although these teas might contain less caffeine than coffee, anyone sensitive to caffeine, or who is nursing or pregnant women, should not consume these teas unless they are decaffeinated.

The ingredients used in green smoothie recipes are similar to those used in juice recipes. When using a juice extractor, however, a significant amount more produce is used to extract a 12- to 16-ounce glass of pure juice as compared to a blended juice. A blended smoothie uses less produce, but to achieve those 12–16 ounces a liquid must be added. When blending or juicing, the entire vegetable or fruit (less seeds, stone, and some skins) should be used. This whole vegetable or fruit gives our bodies the benefits from the phytonutrients found in the skin and flesh of the produce.

Some blender enthusiasts like using the blender for the convenience it provides. Other blender advocates prefer the fiber and convenience of adding protein powders, yogurt, and superfoods to the blender when making drinks. Besides it being faster to make a smoothie, many people feel fuller with blended smoothies as opposed to juicing. If you count yourself among the blender enthusiasts, but prefer a thinner drink without the fiber, you can strain your blended drink using a nut milk filter bag, paint strainer bag, or kitchen strainer.

Older adults don't absorb fiber as well as they did in their younger days, and many men and women don't get enough fiber in their diets to keep their internal systems healthy. Blender fans feel that it is necessary to keep the fiber in their juice so they can obtain enough fiber. A high-fiber soluble diet can lower cholesterol levels and reduce the risk of heart disease and stroke. Consuming fiber in our diets promotes regularity by helping push food through the digestive tract. There are many ways to consume fiber on a daily basis besides blended smoothies. Some of these fibrous foods include salads, quinoa, beans, avocado, whole grains, lentils, pears, artichokes, oatmeal, raspberries, almonds, broccoli, and apples.

Keep in mind that some green smoothie drinks are meant to be a full meal, and you indeed may feel fuller with blended smoothies as compared to pure juice drinks. Regardless, it's important to take your entire day's diet into account when trying to meet your body's nutritional needs and caloric intake. Both juicing and blending have a place in a healthy balanced diet, and both methods provide a delicious and healthy way to increase the amount of micronutrients your body needs every day. It's all up to you whether juicing or blending works best. Viva la difference!

Blend Your Juice!

Purchase a nonprocessed, fresh juice at a juice bar or health food store and pour it into your home blender. Add lemon, ginger, turmeric, apple, banana, more of your favorite greens, and maybe some superfoods. In this way you can increase the portion to a larger drink and have the extra-added nutrients at a lower cost. It is not recommended you purchase commercially made juices found in the cooler section at a grocery store as such drinks are usually processed and pasteurized, and are more than likely to have added sugars. Don't be tricked by the claim "100 percent juice" found on the label. Food companies are allowed to say "100 percent juice" even if there are additives. Some juices have long shelf lives, which can mean a preservative like citric acid or MSG has been added. These juices can do you more harm than good.

THE GOOD NEWS ABOUT GREEN BLENDED SMOOTHIES

As you get comfortable with green blended smoothies you can use less fruit and more vegetables, including celery, cucumber, parsley, cilantro, basil, and sprouts. If in the beginning 2 cups of dark leafy greens are too strong tasting, start by using 1 cup and work your way up. Spinach and romaine are the sweetest dark leafy greens. If you don't like the taste of kale or chard right away, add mint or lemon juice. Remember it's good to switch off your dark leafy greens to get a variety of nutrients.

Healthy Additions to Juices or Blended Smoothies

A number of common food items add flavorful and healthful properties to any juice.

HEALING HERBS

Healing herbs include basil, cinnamon, clove, dill, fennel, mint, and parsley.

ALKALIZING

Kale, cucumbers, celery, red pepper, and spinach promote alkalizing in your body.

DETOXIFYING

Garlic, lemon, ginger, dandelion, stinging nettle, and broccoli all have detoxifying properties.

SWEETENER

Apples, carrots, beets, pears, figs and Medjool dates will add sweetness to your blended drink.

Icy Sweet

· · · · · · · · · · · · · · · · · · ·

Freeze fruits instead of using ice. Ice when blended can dilute a smoothie. If you like a colder drink, simply add ice to your glass instead of the blender.

HEALTHY ADDITIONS

Add any superfood, herb, or spice to your blended drinks, for flavor and health benefits. And for those people who consume dairy, an organic plain, sugarless yogurt may also be added. If you feel a need for some morning protein, you might like to try powders that are dairy, soy, and gluten free; contain no GMOs; and are certified organic.

Green smoothies can be served in a beautiful glass or a Mason jar. They can be decorated with a sprig of mint, a celery stalk, a wedge of fruit, or topped with chopped fruits or nuts. Or sprinkle them with superfoods like maca, cacao powder, hemp seeds, flaxseeds, chia seeds, gogi berries, or blueberries. The ideas are endless.

Items to have freezer ready for smoothies and milkshakes include the following:

- Banana pieces
- Blueberries
- Cranberries
- Mango pieces
- Raspberries
- Pineapple pieces
- Strawberries

INSTRUCTIONS FOR BLENDING

1. Put liquid in blender first so the blade of the blender can work easily with the solid ingredients.
2. Add dark leafy greens and then lightly blend to condense. Next add frozen fruits, then cut-up fresh fruit and vegetables, and lastly superfoods or powders.
3. Start your blender on slow speed then move up to a higher speed.
4. Adding a frozen banana or other frozen fruits will give smoothies a rich thick delicious texture. The addition of ¼ to ½ of an avocado will also help make the smoothie creamy and delicious.
5. If you prefer thicker drinks, add less liquid. If you prefer a thinner drink, add more liquid.
6. Coconut water, green tea, nut or seed milks, or purified water are all good liquid choices.
7. For a slightly sweeter smoothie, use a couple drops of stevia or a Medjool date or two.

Serving Size

· · · · · · · · · · · · · · · · · · ·

The smoothie recipes serve one.

FRESH KICK DAN

Energy boosting, cleansing, and alkalizing. A wide variety of vitamins and nutrients complete this smoothie. Loaded with vitamins A, D, E, and K, this smoothie is a great source of omega-3 fatty acid. Anticancer, nourishing to the eyes, and just the right amount of good fat to balance everything out.

INGREDIENTS

½ cup filtered water or coconut water

1 handful spinach

2 tomatoes, seeds removed

2-inch piece fresh turmeric or ¼ teaspoon ground

3 parsley sprigs

½ of an avocado

½ lemon, juiced

A grind or two of black pepper

A pinch of pink Himalayan salt

A pinch of cayenne pepper

More water or coconut water as needed

DIRECTIONS

Blend all ingredients in order listed in a high-speed blender.

HAWAIIAN PUNCH ME

Skin purifier, digestion facilitator, and hydration booster. This smoothie contains health-promoting compounds, including minerals and vitamins that are essential for optimum health. It will help remove harmful inflammatory free radicals from the body. It will also help to maintain healthy mucus membranes and control heart rate and blood pressure. Drink this for better vision and skin.

INGREDIENTS

1 cup coconut water, filtered water, or nut milk

1 handful dark leafy greens of choice

½ cup pineapple

2 carrots, scrubbed and chopped

1-inch piece of ginger, peeled

DIRECTIONS

Blend all ingredients in order listed in a high-speed blender.

COUNTRY C

Glowing skin, antioxidant rich, and cleansing. This smoothie is a salad in a glass. Greens help bring balance to your body. Calming kale and vitamin C will help fight inflammation and disease.

INGREDIENTS

¾ cup filtered water

2 kale leaves, stems removed

½ red sweet pepper

A small bud of broccoli, broken into pieces

1 cup pineapple

1 tomato, seeds removed

Pepper flakes to taste

Pinch of pink Himalayan salt

DIRECTIONS

Blend all ingredients in order listed in a high-speed blender.

URBAN C

Cancer fighting, pain relieving, and antiaging. This winning combination is a rich source of antioxidants. It can eliminate oxidative stress, prevent premature aging, and help cure headaches and migraines.

INGREDIENTS

½ cup coconut water

1 handful spinach

1 cup or more frozen cherries

1 orange

1 kiwi, cut in half and fruit scooped out

DIRECTIONS

Blend all ingredients in order listed in a high-speed blender.

THE WARRIOR

Digestive aid, detoxifiing, and hydrating. This smoothie will bring your body into balance, aid in digestion, detoxify the body, calm inflammation, improve metabolism, and support kidney function.

INGREDIENTS

½ cup filtered water or coconut water

1 grapefruit, juiced

1 handful spinach

2 celery stalks, cut into chunks

½ medium cucumber, cut into chunks

1 green apple, cored

1-inch piece ginger, peeled

DIRECTIONS

Blend all ingredients in order listed in a high-speed blender.

ABCDEFG

Kidney cleansing, antioxidant rich, and detoxifying. Benefits of this smoothie include cancer prevention, kidney and liver improvement, blood pressure lowering, weight balancing, and cardiovascular conditioning.

INGREDIENTS

¾ cup filtered water or more if needed

1 apple

½ cup blueberries

3 celery stalks

½ cup daikon

1 handful parsley

¼ cup fennel

1-inch piece of ginger

DIRECTIONS

Blend all ingredients in order listed in a high-speed blender.

LEMONADE-APPLE

Anti-inflammatory, immune building, and metabolism balancing. High in iron and vitamin K. Kale has shown to help protect against various cancers. This simple smoothie is filled with antioxidants and helps to manages cardiovascular problems. Pineapple is a natural anti-inflammatory and can help lower blood pressure, decrease age related macular degeneration, and help to combat free radicals known to cause cancer.

INGREDIENTS

1–1½ cups filtered water

3 kale leaves, stems removed

2 green apples, cored

1 lemon, juiced

1 cup pineapple, chopped

3 mint sprigs

DIRECTIONS

Blend all ingredients in order listed in a high-speed blender.

MACK BLISS

Age-defying, circulation building, and cancer fighting. As we age, our body's natural defenses against free radicals and oxidative stress become less effective. Researchers believe that a high level of dietary antioxidants can prevent many age-related diseases. Strawberries, blueberries, raspberries, and blackberries are good for circulation and can help keep the heart and eyes healthy. Antioxidants can also help fight chronic diseases including cancer.

INGREDIENTS

1–1½ cups filtered water, coconut water, or almond milk

1 handful dark leafy greens of your choice

1 cup fresh or frozen blueberries

1 cup fresh or frozen strawberries

½ lemon, juiced

3 mint sprigs

2–3 dates, stevia to taste, or sweetener of choice (optional)

DIRECTIONS

Blend all ingredients in order listed in a high-speed blender.

PINEAPPLE MINT JULEP

Anti-inflammatory, improved circulation and purifying. Rich in detoxifying properties, antioxidants, and vitamins A, C, K, and E. Strengthens immune system, lowers blood pressure, supports cardiovascular skin and bone health. Increases brain function.

INGREDIENTS

1–1½ cups filtered water

1 handful dark leafy greens of your choice

1 cup pineapple

1 ripe pear, cored and chopped

Handful of grapes

2 mint sprigs

1 lemon, juiced

DIRECTIONS

Blend all ingredients in order listed in a high-speed blender.

SWEET ME

Eye support, cancer fighter, and skin purifier. This smoothie may help to alleviate joint pain, arthritis, tumor growth, and the healing of skin wounds. High in potassium, which is associated with reducing the risk of stroke. Protects bone mineral density and reduces the formation of kidney stones.

INGREDIENTS

1–1½ cups filtered water or coconut water

1 handful spinach

½ banana, frozen

½ cup pineapple

1 cup strawberries, frozen

DIRECTIONS

Blend all ingredients in order listed in a high-speed blender.

COLOR ME RACHEL

Antioxidant rich, anti-inflammatory, and skin healing. High antioxidants can fight free radicals, and with beta-carotene and minerals, including copper, zinc, and folate, your body will achieve its natural healthy state and get your creative juices flowing! Enzymes in pineapple can reduce bruising, swelling, and healing time post-surgery. Vitamin C plays a role in the formation of collagen, the support system of your skin.

INGREDIENTS

1½ cups filtered water, coconut water, or almond milk

3 kale leaves, stems removed

Small handful parsley

½ cup pineapple

½ cup berries, fresh or frozen

1 green apple, cored

DIRECTIONS

Blend all ingredients in order listed in a high-speed blender.

BLEND ME

Clarity increasing, anti-oxidant rich, and mood boosting. Packs energy into your day and is great before a strenuous workout. Helps to relieve muscle cramps during workouts. Builds strong bones and improves PMS symptoms as it relieves stress and helps with relaxation. Aids in weight loss and protects against heart attack and stroke.

INGREDIENTS

1 cup coconut water

½ cup raspberries

½ cup blueberries

1 banana, frozen

1-inch piece ginger

DIRECTIONS

Blend all ingredients in order listed in a high-speed blender.

ENERGIZE ME

Metabolism booster, immune supporter, and digestive balancer. Builds strong bones and teeth, and strengthens your nervous system. High levels of vitamin B6 reduces swelling and protects against type 2 diabetes. Cuts down on inflammation of the blood vessels, which aids in the prevention of heart attacks and strokes.

INGREDIENTS

1½ cups almond milk or coconut water

1 cup spinach leaves

½ banana, frozen

1 lime, juiced

½ fresh vanilla bean or ½ teaspoon vanilla extract

2 teaspoons honey, maple syrup, or sweetener of choice to taste

DIRECTIONS

Blend all ingredients in order listed in a high-speed blender.

GREEN ME

Antioxidant rich, metabolic boosting, and blood pressure regulating. Grapes may dramatically reduce your cells ability to store fat. Resveratrol, which is found in grapes, can protect your heart and improve the dilation of blood vessels. When blood flows easily through vessels, the walls of the blood vessels relax, resulting in a significant reduction in heart-attack risk factors.

INGREDIENTS

1½ cups green tea

1 cup spinach

1 cup green seedless grapes

1 banana, frozen

DIRECTIONS

Blend all ingredients in order listed in a high-speed blender.

CLEANSE ME

Detoxifying, cell repairing, and cholesterol lowering. Rich in vitamins A, C, K, and B12, which helps your immune system get strong. Bones and nervous system will improve while excess fluids are flushed from the body. This smoothie may help your blood pressure while toning the heart. Anti-inflammatory properties can encourage digestion and relax stiff muscles.

INGREDIENTS

1–1½ cups filtered water or green tea

1 cup spinach

½ bunch parsley

1 cup pineapple

1 celery stalk, chopped

DIRECTIONS

Blend all ingredients in order listed in a high-speed blender.

CHANGE ME

Cancer reducer, heart helper, and weight balancer. Boost your energy level, lose weight, and get rid of fatigue with grapefruit. This smoothie will improve digestion and bowel excretion. It also protects your heart, lowers insulin levels, and suppresses your appetite. Broccoli can help with cancer prevention, reduce cholesterol, create bone health and is a powerful antioxidant. If you don't care for broccoli, don't fret because the taste is masked in this smoothie with grapefruit and banana.

INGREDIENTS

1 cup almond milk

1 pink grapefruit

1 frozen banana

1 cup broccoli, chopped

DIRECTIONS

Blend all ingredients in order listed in a high-speed blender.

LOVE ME

Anti-inflammatory, beauty building, and alkaline forming. Heart-healthy lettuce is loaded with vitamin C and beta-carotene. These pals work together to prevent the oxidation of cholesterol, which prevents the buildup of arterial plaque. Minerals remove toxins and keep our acid/alkaline balance in order. Look for clearer thinking, improved skin, and better sleep.

INGREDIENTS

1 cup desired liquid, coconut water, green tea, or hemp seeds

4 romaine leaves

2 ripe pears, cored

½ fennel blub

½ lime, juiced

DIRECTIONS

Blend all ingredients in order listed in a high-speed blender.

FORGET-ME-NOT

Hydrating, purifying, and infection fighting. Cranberries are a rich source of flavonoids, which can inhibit the development of breast and colon cancers. Other benefits consist of heart, mouth, and stomach health. We can never be too hydrated, and cucumber and celery will keep you on track.

INGREDIENTS

1 cup filtered water, or more if needed

1 large handful spinach

1 cucumber, chopped

1 stalk celery, chopped

1 apple, cored

1 pear, cored

½ cup cranberries

DIRECTIONS

Blend all ingredients in order listed in a high-speed blender.

GET READY

Digestive cleanser, antioxidant rich, and immune strengthener. Vitamin C is a powerful antioxidant, which is known to help prevent neurodegenerative diseases and arthritis, and promote heart health. Spinach is loaded with vitamins A, D, E, K, and a host of trace minerals. Spinach is also a good source of omega-3 fatty acids, which may help prevent arthritis. Researchers claim there are more than a dozen different flavonoid compounds in spinach, which function as anticancer and anti-inflammatory agents. Maintaining an alkaline body is important for overall health and spinach is an alkalizing leafy green, which will help with the prevention of obesity and many other health problems, including protection against eye diseases and strengthening of bone.

INGREDIENTS

1 cup coconut water, almond milk or green tea

1 cup spinach or dark leafy greens of choice

1 banana, frozen

1 cup strawberries

2 tangerines, juiced

DIRECTIONS

Blend all ingredients in order listed in a high-speed blender.

PURPLE HAZE

Brain building, beautifying, and detoxifying. The content of vitamin C and sulfur in cabbage helps to remove toxins and uric acid, which are the main causes of rheumatism, arthritis, gout, and skin disease. Grapes greatly improve the dilation of blood vessels. And cancer-fighting cranberries also fight heart disease, remove plaque, help prevent stroke and hardening of the arteries. Throw in the fact that cranberries contain citric acid and other nutrients that are known to prevent kidney stones and bladder problems. Eating cranberries is a healthy habit to get into to promote antiaging and weight loss.

INGREDIENTS

1½ cups filtered water or coconut water

½ cup purple cabbage

1 cup purple seedless grapes

½ cup cranberries

1 orange, juiced

DIRECTIONS

Blend all ingredients in order listed in a high-speed blender.

GREEN GODDESS GIGI

Protein rich, heart healthy, and blood pressure and cholesterol lowering. The benefits are a multitude of vitamins A, B6, D, E, K, and a host of trace minerals, including copper, iron, magnesium, and potassium, which will help maintain a healthy heart and lower cholesterol and blood pressure levels. Anti-inflammatory properties promote eye health, with an excellent source of carotenoid lutein, which is known to help protect age-related cataracts and macular degeneration.

INGREDIENTS

1½ cups almond milk or green tea

1 handful spinach

1 orange, juiced

½ avocado

1 banana, frozen

2 Medjool dates, honey, or maple syrup to taste

DIRECTIONS

Blend all ingredients in order listed in a high-speed blender.

RED LANTERN

Detoxifying, stress fighting, and antioxidant boosting. Removing toxins and heavy metals will help your body heal quickly. High in vitamins A, B6, and C, count on Red Lantern to deliver a high quality of nutrients. Powerful antioxidant cranberries help prevent arthritis, urinary tract infections, memory loss, and may reverse the effects of aging.

INGREDIENTS

1–1½ cups almond milk, filtered water, or coconut water

1 red apple, cored

¼ red bell pepper

1 blood orange, juiced

1 cup cranberries

DIRECTIONS

Blend all ingredients in order listed in a high-speed blender.

SUNSET

Protein builder, antioxidant booster, and cancer fighter. A combination of protein, vitamins, and minerals can have many cures. Vitamin A can promote good eyesight and prevent night blindness. Vitamin C will support the immune system and antioxidant compounds may protect against colon, prostate, and breast cancers.

INGREDIENTS

1½ cups hemp milk or coconut water

1 cup mango or papaya, fresh or frozen

1 yellow apple, cored

1 kiwi, cut in half and fruit scooped out

¼ yellow sweet pepper

½ lemon, juiced

DIRECTIONS

Blend all ingredients in order listed in a high-speed blender.

BLUEBERRY BLAST OFF

Antioxidant boosting, mood elevating, and antiaging. Vitamin E and trace minerals supply antiaging properties, and with more than ten essential amino acids, count on healthy hair, nails, and glowing skin. Get protected from breast, colon, and prostate cancers with this smoothie. Look for improvement in lowering cholesterol, balancing blood sugar, and decreasing hot flashes.

INGREDIENTS

1 cup coconut water or liquid of choice

2 teaspoons hemp seeds

1 cup blueberries, frozen

1 cup spinach

½ banana, frozen

1 tablespoon raw cacao powder

More water as necessary for consistency

DIRECTIONS

Blend all ingredients in order listed in a high-speed blender.

ON THE MONEY MIKE

Heart healthy, cholesterol lowering, and toxic flushing. Packed full of essential vitamins, including A, C, K, B1, B2, and B6, and minerals, including manganese, potassium, iron, magnesium, calcium, phosphorous, and copper, this smoothie is right on the money to bring ultimate health. Look for better eyesight, a healthy urinary and gastrointestinal tract, and lower cholesterol.

INGREDIENTS

1 cup filtered water, coconut water, or hemp seed milk

6 romaine leaves

1 Granny Smith (green) apple, cored

1 stalk celery, chopped

½ cucumber, chopped

1 orange, juiced

DIRECTIONS

Blend all ingredients in order listed in a high-speed blender.

LET IT BEET

Kidney cleanser, circulation improver, and cardio-vascular supporter. Give your gallbladder and liver a little love, build up the red corpuscles, and stimulate the lymphatic system throughout the body with the right combination of vitamins and minerals. Add some extra vitamin C to help prevent the risk of developing prostrate and other cancers and get a bonus of detoxification of the body. Drink up and you will help to fight oxygen free radicals (which damage cells), lower cholesterol, and support a healthy immune system.

INGREDIENTS

1–1½ cups filtered water

1 handful dark leafy greens

2 beet leaves

½ beetroot, peeled

½ pink grapefruit, juiced

1 carrot, scrubbed and cut in chunks

1-inch piece ginger, peeled

DIRECTIONS

Blend all ingredients in order listed in a high-speed blender.

LADY AUDREY

Potassium rich, blood pressure lowering, and anti-aging. Protects from varying cancers, Alzheimer's, and autoimmune disorders. Powerful antioxidants can help prevent memory loss, aid in joint flexibility, and reduce the risk of cataracts, macular degeneration, and arthritis. Take advantage of the daily-required nutrients, including A, C, beta-carotene, magnesium, flavonoids, and electrolytes.

INGREDIENTS

1–1½ cups coconut water or hemp milk

5 kale leaves, stems removed

1 cup cranberries

1 cup red seedless grapes

1 orange, juiced

DIRECTIONS

Blend all ingredients in order listed in a high-speed blender.

ECO FUEL

Anti-inflammatory, digestive supporting, and antioxidant rich. Keep immune system healthy, build collagen, and support blood vessels, skin, tendons, and ligaments. Antioxidants can help prevent memory loss, aid in joint flexibility, and help reduce cataracts, macular degeneration, and arthritis. Replenish electrolytes, while improving metabolism and supplying energy to the body and cells.

INGREDIENTS

1½ cups coconut water

2 cups dark leafy greens

2 kiwis, cut in half and fruit scooped out

½ cup of fresh or frozen strawberries

½ cup of fresh or frozen pineapple

½ lemon, peeled and seeded

DIRECTIONS

Blend all ingredients in order listed in a high-speed blender.

GAME ON

Collagen builder, mood balancer, cell protector, and nutrient builder. A, C, E, K, iron, calcium, potassium, and phosphorus reduce blood pressure, lower cholesterol, and help keep the immune system healthy. Feel calm and notice glowing skin while keeping hydrated. A unique combination of antioxidants helps protect the cell DNA from oxidative damage, which in turn can help prevent cancer. Vitamin C has been proven to boost the immune system while performing anticlotting benefits.

INGREDIENTS

1½ cups filtered water, coconut water, or almond milk

2 cups spinach or dark leafy greens of choice

1 cup mango, fresh or frozen

1 cup pineapple

1 banana, frozen

DIRECTIONS

Blend all ingredients in order listed in a high-speed blender.

HIGH FIVE

Digestive aid, antioxidant protection, and heart defense. Protects eyes from macular degeneration and other eye problems with kiwis' high levels of lutein and zeaxanthin, which are both natural chemicals found in the human eye. Kiwi is alkalizing and protects the skin from degeneration. Powerful antioxidants in grapes help the body rid itself from free radicals, which make them a good antiaging fruit. Add in the powerful nutrient in romaine leaves and enjoy the essential vitamins, including A, C, B1, B6, and K. Include the minerals manganese, potassium, iron, magnesium, calcium, copper, and phosphorus and you will know that you are taking good care of your health.

INGREDIENTS

1–1½ cups filtered water or coconut water

3 romaine lettuce leaves

1 cup red or green seedless grapes

2 kiwis, cut in half and fruit scooped out

1 orange, juiced

DIRECTIONS

Blend all ingredients in order listed in a high-speed blender.

FALL

Protein enrichment, anti-inflammatory, and infection protection. This smoothie is a combination of healthy protein that contains essential amino acids and fatty acids, which are necessary to maintain a healthy body. Add in detoxifying apples, cranberries to help protect the urinary tract from infection, an orange to help prevent various cancers and lower cholesterol. Put in some dark leafy greens to round out nutrients and vitamins, and this smoothie may just make your day a little brighter.

INGREDIENTS

1–1½ cups almond, hemp, or other nut milk

1 apple, cored

1 cup of cranberries

1 orange, juiced

A handful dark leafy greens

Pinch of pumpkin pie spice, or a combination of cinnamon, nutmeg, allspice, and cloves

DIRECTIONS

Blend all ingredients in order listed in a high-speed blender.

THE RUSH

Cleansing, digestion promoting, and immune supporting. Papaya contains papain, which is an enzyme that helps with digestion. This antioxidant-rich, nutrient-dense smoothie promotes cardiovascular health and cancer protection. It has anti-inflammatory effects and helps in the prevention of age-related macular degeneration. If you are working on lowering your blood pressure, adding celery to smoothies is recommended. Potassium, magnesium, calcium, copper, and protein round out this potent nutrient-dense smoothie.

INGREDIENTS

1–1½ cups filtered water, coconut water, or almond milk

1 cup dark leafy greens

1 celery stalk, chopped

1 cup papaya, fresh or frozen

½ banana, frozen

DIRECTIONS

Blend all ingredients in order listed in a high-speed blender.

TOWER OF POWER

Hydrating, collagen building, and anti-inflammatory supporting. Kale has more iron than beef, and with fewer calories. Parsley can neutralize particular types of carcinogens such as cigarettes or charcoal grill smoke. The flavonoids in parsley help prevent oxygen-based damage to cells. Hydrating cucumber and cholesterol-lowering celery, along with potassium-rich, anti-inflammatory, digestive- and collagen-building pineapple, can add immune building, blood pressure lowering, and potassium to this smoothie.

INGREDIENTS

1½ cups coconut water or nut milk of choice

2 kale leaves, stems removed

1 celery stalk, chopped

½ cucumber, chopped

2 parsley stems with leaves

1 cup pineapple

½ lemon, juiced

DIRECTIONS

Blend all ingredients in order listed in a high-speed blender.

THE GLOW

Cholesterol lowering, anticancer supporting, and antioxidant rich. Lycopene in tomatoes helps to protect cells and harmful oxygen-free radicals. Tomatoes are very high in antioxidants, which have shown to support antiaging. Carrot's anticancer properties may reduce the risk of breast or colon cancers. Heart, respiratory, and urinary tract health; protection for eyes, teeth, and gums; and hydration are just a few of the benefits of this smoothie.

INGREDIENTS

1–1½ cups filtered water or coconut water

6 romaine leaves

2 celery stalks, chopped

1 carrot, scrubbed and chopped

1 tomato, seeded

½ cucumber, chopped

DIRECTIONS

Blend all ingredients in order listed in a high-speed blender.

PURIFY

Cleansing, protein building, and anti-inflammatory. Nut or seed milks supply protein with little fat. Flaxseeds protect against breast, colon, and prostrate cancers. This smoothie can decrease hot flashes, lower cholesterol, improve blood sugar levels, and protect against radiation. Pears are a high source of dietary fiber. They contain magnesium, potassium, calcium, and copper. Pears lower the risk of macular degeneration and are linked to prevention of osteoporosis.

INGREDIENTS

1 cup almond or hemp seed milk

2 pears, cored and roughly cut

1 tablespoon flaxseeds

Good pinch of cardamom

DIRECTIONS

Blend all ingredients in order listed in a high-speed blender.

RENEW

Cancer fighting, detoxifying, and stimulating. Detoxifying takes place when blending a variety of vegetables together. Enzymes are stimulated and carcinogens are neutralized. Hydration is never overstated and very important for ultimate health. Benefits of these ingredients include anti-inflammatory properties, free radical protection, and cancer cell inhibition. Arthritis-related problems respond well to this smoothie.

INGREDIENTS

1 cup filtered water

1 grapefruit, juiced

2 chard leaves, stems removed

4 parsley sprigs

1 celery stalk, cut in pieces

¼ cucumber, cut in pieces

1-inch piece of ginger, peeled

DIRECTIONS

Blend all ingredients in order listed in a high-speed blender.

RELAX

Stress management, antioxidant rich, and immune building. Manage blood pressure and keep electrolytes in balance. Antioxidants help to protect the cell DNA from oxidative damage, which in turn can help prevent cancer. Strawberries can help lower cholesterol, reverse some effects from aging, lower blood pressure, and prevent some cancers. Stress release is important to keep our cells healthy. Slowly sip this smoothie for best results.

INGREDIENTS

1 cup filtered water, almond milk, or coconut water

2 cups dark leafy greens

2 kiwis peeled or cut in half and fruit scooped out

1 cup strawberries

½ banana, frozen

5 mint sprigs

DIRECTIONS

Blend all ingredients in order listed in a high-speed blender.

WILD SIDE

Alkalizing, skin cleansing, and cholesterol lowering. One cup of mango supplies 25 percent of our daily needed vitamin A. Vitamin A is known to promote good eyesight and help to prevent night blindness. Vitamin C, with its abundant enzymes, may help to lower serum cholesterol levels. Many fruits and vegetables contain antioxidant compounds, which have been found to protect against breast, colon, prostate, and leukemia cancers. These powerful antioxidants may also prevent memory loss and the effects of aging.

INGREDIENTS

1–1½ cups coconut milk (see page 186 for recipe)

1 large handful of greens of your choice

1 mango, frozen or fresh, cut in chunks

½ cup strawberries

1 banana frozen, cut in pieces

DIRECTIONS

Blend all ingredients in order listed in a high-speed blender.

LION HEARTED

Antioxidant rich, brain booster, and energy booster. Using green tea in smoothies is a brilliant addition. Although green tea contains some caffeine—not as much as coffee—it is proven to have many health benefits. It is fat burning, boosts metabolic rate, and gives you energy. High in antioxidants, green tea is an excellent source to help reduce breast, prostate, and colorectal cancers. Studies show that catechin compounds in green tea have protective effects on neurons, potentially lowering the risk of Alzheimer's and Parkinson's. Green tea improves dental health and lowers the risks of infections. Add green tea to any smoothie recipe in place of other liquids.

INGREDIENTS

1 cup green tea

½ cup almond milk

1 cup frozen blueberries

1 frozen banana, cut in pieces

1 teaspoon honey or 3 Medjool dates

DIRECTIONS

Blend all ingredients in order listed in a high-speed blender.

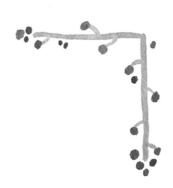

BRIGHT LIGHT

Anti-stress, antiaging, and eyesight building. Helps prevent degenerative diseases, strengthens your bones and teeth, encourages collagen production, and helps to cope with stress. That's what you get when you add a good source of vitamin C to your smoothie. Toss in some vitamin D to support your immune system, energy levels, mood, nerves, heart, and skin and you are on your way to better health. This smoothie also contains a good source of magnesium, which is a relaxation and antistress mineral, and it will improve your arteries, blood, bones, and heart.

INGREDIENTS

1–1½ almond milk, hemp milk, or coconut water

½ cup sweet potato, peeled and cut into chunks

1 carrot, scrubbed and cut into chunks

1 small piece of ginger

Pinch of cinnamon

DIRECTIONS

Blend all ingredients in order listed in a high-speed blender.

YOU SAY TOMATO

Eyesight building, antioxidant protecting, and cholesterol controlling. Lower blood pressure, support eye health, and receive a large dose of vitamins and minerals.

Hydration is key in a healthy body, and celery adds this to the mix. A little garlic never hurt anybody; in fact, it's recommended for regulating diabetes by lowering blood sugars. It contains B6, which is good for our immune system, and aids in the prevention of multiple types of cancers, including prostate, breast, bladder, colon, and stomach.

INGREDIENTS

1–1½ cups filtered water or green tea

2 tomatoes, seeds removed

2 celery stalks, cut in chunks

1 carrot, scrubbed and cut into chunks

1 garlic clove

Small handful parsley

Pinch of salt

DIRECTIONS

Blend all ingredients in order listed in a high-speed blender.

GOOD FOR EVERYBODY

Antioxidant rich, detoxifying, and mood balancing. Reduce intestinal disorders, diverticulitis, and some types of cancers. Vitamin B can help balance moods swings. Vitamin C, potassium, and magnesium are all contained in one smoothie. Lowering blood pressure, detoxifying, and mood balancing are all supported by high antioxidant compounds. Even your dogs will feel better when you add a little into their food.

INGREDIENTS

1–1½ cups filtered water

1 handful spinach

½ banana

½ apple, cored and cut into pieces

¼ cup sweet potato, peeled and cut into chunks

Handful of berries

1 heaping teaspoon almond butter

DIRECTIONS

Blend all ingredients in order listed in a high-speed blender.

Hemp Seed Milk, page 190
Chocolate Almond Milk, page 188
Almond Milk, page 185

BASIC NUT MILK AND MILKSHAKE RECIPES

Nut and seed milk smoothies are lactose and gluten free. Nuts like almonds, Brazil nuts, hazelnuts, cashews, and seeds all make delicious milks.

Some decades ago, for most Americans the only milk choices were whole, 2%, or skim. Back then milk came mostly from cows. Mooo . . . ve over cow, it's about time you got a much-needed rest. If you've seen any happy cows lately, it's because times have changed, the choices have widened, and cow's milk is being replaced with alternative milks.

Milkshake smoothies are simply delicious when made with a base of nut or seed milks. Raw nut milks can also be used to make ice creams, pies, cream sauces, and nut-based dairy-free cheeses. These milks can also be used on cereals or in lattes.

About the New Milks

Nut and seed milks are easy to make at home, and make a perfect base for smoothies (see pages 185, 186, 190 for recipes). If you are lactose intolerant or have vegan dietary restrictions, it is in your best interest to learn how to make your own milks. Almond milk has become the most popular alternative to dairy or soymilk. It contains fewer calories than dairy or soy milk, has no saturated fats or cholesterol, and supplies about 25 percent of our daily vitamin D and about half of our vitamin E. If you are buying almond milk at your supermarket and not making it at home, be sure to read the label for sugars, salt, or other additives. Remember that almond milk purchased

at your supermarket is industrially processed. If you purchase almond milk at a supermarket, look for unsweetened organic varieties.

Although soymilk has a protein value that is close to cow's milk, soy itself is not without its controversy. In recent years claims have been made that link phytoestrogen-rich soy to increased risks of breast cancer. Other research shows that soy is disruptive to our hormones because soy is one of the most genetically modified foods on the market today. Soy is heavily sprayed with chemicals, and because of these chemicals, soy is grown in depleted soils. Consumers with gastritis or irritable bowel syndrome should stay away from soy as it can cause bloating. People with tumors and hormonal issues should also stay away from soy. If you are going to buy soy milk, consume it in moderation and choose unflavored, organic varieties.

Another milk replacement is rice milk. Rice milk, however, is processed. It's milled and blended with water. During this process carbohydrates become sugar, which gives rice milk its sweet taste. Rice milk is low in nutrients. It might be an alternative for people who are lactose intolerant, but it has twice the amount of carbohydrates as cow's milk.

If you decide to stick with cow's milk, purchase organic. The labeling should read BHT free or rBHT free. BHT is bovine growth hormone. One wonders

about the reports that say the United States has one of the highest rates of osteoporosis in the world. Could this be true because Americans consume the largest amount of dairy products in the world? Could it be that cow's milk—even organic cow's milk— provides few real benefits? The Department of Health and Exercise Science at Colorado State University claims that milk is the cause of spiked insulin levels and may increase the risk of prostate cancer. They also claim this white carbohydrate can be harmful because of its high glycemic index, which in turn causes the blood sugar or glucose to rise after drinking just an 8-ounce glass. A sudden increase of insulin in the bloodstream causes a sudden drop in glucose levels that may result in increased hunger. The body's reactions to this can also cause fatigue, increase fat around the midsection, and may speed up aging.

Raw nut and seed milks are low-calorie and high-nutrient alternatives to dairy, soy, and rice milks. For example, raw almond milk contains vitamin E, potassium, copper, and magnesium while being low in calories (an 8-ounce portion contains approximately 70 calories). Nut and seed milk smoothies are lactose and gluten free and contain no saturated fats. Nuts like almonds, Brazil nuts, hazelnuts, cashews, and seeds such as hemp all make delicious milks.

Nut Pulp

See page 298 for ideas on using nut pulp

ALMOND MILK

Only 60 calories for an 8-ounce glass, and there's no cholesterol or saturated fat so it's heart healthy.

INGREDIENTS

1 cup almonds, soaked overnight

3½ cups filtered water (more if you prefer a thinner milk)

2 Medjool dates, pitted

½ teaspoon vanilla extract

DIRECTIONS

Strain soaked almonds and rinse well. Soaking releases the enzyme inhibitors and makes for easier digestion. Place nuts in high-speed blender and add water, dates, and vanilla, and process until smooth. Place a nut milk filter bag or paint strainer bag over a bowl, and then pour the almond milk into the bag. With one hand hold the top of the bag, and with the other hand proceed to squeeze all the milk from the bag into the bowl. If you don't have a bag, a wire strainer or cheesecloth will work, but a bag makes the job easier. A nut milk filter bag can be purchased online and paint strainer bags can be found at your local hardware store. Both of these items can be found on my website, YoungOnRawFood.com. Once all the liquid is squeezed into the bowl, pour it into a large glass container with a screw-top lid, such as a Mason jar, and store in the refrigerator. Milk will last about 3 to 4 days.

CASHEW MILK

Cashews are high in the amino acid tryptophan, which helps to make serotonin. Cashews make creamy, rich-tasting milk with only 72 calories in an 8-ounce glass.

INGREDIENTS

1 cup cashews, soaked 3 to 4 hours

3½ cups filtered water (more if you prefer a thinner milk)

2 Medjool dates, pitted

½ teaspoon vanilla extract

DIRECTIONS

Strain soaked cashews and rinse well. Soaking releases the enzyme inhibitors and makes for easier digestion. Place nuts in high-speed blender and add water, dates, and vanilla, and process until smooth. Cashew milk does not have to be strained. Pour into a glass container with a screw-top lid, such as a Mason jar, and store in the refrigerator. Will last about 3 to 4 days.

Faster Cashew "Milk"

A handful of soaked cashews can be put directly into the blender along with other fruits and vegetables without making cashew milk. Add appropriate amount of water to blend.

COCONUT MILK

If you make your own coconut milk from young Thai coconuts, the meat is around 140 calories and the water is very low in calories and has no fat. The health benefits are many. Commercial coconut milk has a very high calorie count and is worth staying away from.

INGREDIENTS

1–2 young Thai coconuts, use both meat and water

(Will yield approximately 2–3 cups coconut milk.)

DIRECTIONS

You have to break open a coconut to make the milk. A young Thai coconut, both the water and meat, is the best coconut to use because it is chock-full of healthy nutrients. Once you get the hang of opening the coconut, you will find it easy. There are special tools to open young Thai coconuts, which can be found online. Many health food markets will open them for you in the produce department.

Young Thai coconuts are white, fibrous, and cone-shaped. They come wrapped in clear plastic, which should be removed before starting the opening process. There are several methods to open the coconut. Using a cleaver may seem threatening at first, but it is one of the best methods to use. The butt end, closest to the handle, of a very large strong knife will also work fine. If using the kitchen counter, place a dishtowel underneath the coconut for a safe, nonslip surface. Always place the coconut on a firm surface before opening.

When using a cleaver there is no need to remove the white husk at the top, as the cleaver will penetrate through. When using a large knife, it's best to remove the white husk around the top of the coconut.

Place the coconut on its side and slice a section of the husk off from the edge to the tip. Turn the coconut as you go, taking off a section at a time until you see the signs of the brownish hard shell. When the husk on top has been removed, set the coconut upright. Strike the butt of the knife a couple inches from the center point of the coconut. Go around the top in the same manner until you have made a circle.

There is always one soft spot when striking around the circle. This soft spot is the point where you will eventually lift off the shell circle. Sometimes after a few strikes, coconut water will squirt out of the soft spot. Continue holding the knife in one hand and using the butt end of the knife, being very mindful of your hands at all times, strike around the circle again.

It is best not to have your hand on the coconut when first starting out. Slowly continue around by striking firmly through the shell. If you are using a cleaver, you will strike less in each area before breaking through. A knife will take more strikes than a cleaver. Be sure to strike firmly.

Once you have loosened through the shell around your pattern, the top should easily lift off. Do not use the tip of your knife to lift off the top piece as it could break the knife tip, only use the butt end. Insert the butt end and wedge the top off.

Once you have the lid off, pour the water through a strainer into a bowl or directly into blender. To remove the coconut meat, use a large tablespoon, and insert the backside of the spoon between the shell and the coconut meat. The backside of the spoon should be on the outside of the coconut meat closest to the shell. Slowly go around the opening with your spoon, loosening the meat from the shell. Remove any hard shell that sticks to the white coconut meat. This can usually be done by scraping with a spoon or small sharp knife.

When all the meat is removed from the shell, rinse and place coconut meat in a high-speed blender along with the coconut water. Blend un-

til completely smooth. To remove any small shell pieces, strain mixture. You now have coconut milk.

Every coconut can be different when it comes to the meat. Some meat is very soft and rubbery, and others very thick, hard, and dry. Both are good. The tougher coconut meat takes more time to blend and most times needs straining. The coconut meat should be white without coloration, including blue or purple. A very light pink is okay, but nothing darker. Dispose of discolored coconuts, both water and meat, and do not consume. Coconut water and meat can be frozen when separated from the outer shell. Coconut meat has many other uses, including desserts and breads.

For all milkshakes, add more liquid to thin, or less for a thicker shake.

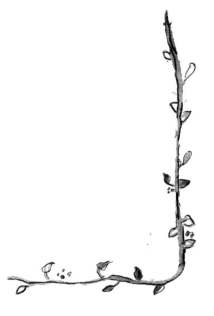

CHOCOLATE ALMOND MILK

Cacao powder and cacao nibs are a great source of magnesium, which plays a role in muscle function, circulation, and bone strength.

INGREDIENTS

1½ cups almond milk
(see page 185 for basic Almond Milk recipe)

3–4 tablespoons cacao powder
(more if you like it richer)

2–3 tablespoons maple syrup or 4–5 dates

DIRECTIONS

Blend all ingredients adding maple syrup or dates to taste. Refrigerate to chill.

Complete Guide to Milkshakes

Modern milkshakes are delicious and nutritious. In the past, milkshakes were thought of as a dessert. In some places they still are. Milkshakes are also known for being high in empty calories and saturated fat. Milkshakes are traditionally made with dairy milk, cream, and ice cream. These milkshakes also contain thirty or more grams of sugar. Many milkshakes like these are not made with fresh fruits, but are instead flavored with sugary syrups and juice concentrates. This is the kind of milkshake you might find at fast food or chain restaurants.

THE GOOD NEWS ABOUT MILKSHAKES

The modern milkshake recipes provided in this book are made with whole produce. In these milkshakes, plant-based milks, fruits, coconut meat, and natural flavors are the primary ingredients. If you follow these recipes you will use frozen or fresh organic fruits, including bananas, berries, mangoes, and stone fruits. You will not add sugary syrups. These milkshakes are sweet but have nutritional value and are high in dietary fibers, vitamins, and antioxidants.

Milkshakes may contain nut or seed milks, coconut milk, coconut water, green tea, or citrus juice. A milkshake can be filling and may be used for a meal replacer if you have added enough healthy ingredients to it. A boost of herbs or tinctures may be added for extra nutrients. Protein powders may also be added.

Proteins, in the form of raw dairy and gluten-free powders, may be added to the base liquid, which is comprised of nut and seed milks, green tea, coconut milk, or coconut water (see pages 185, 186, 190 for nut, seed, and coconut milk recipes). These milkshakes can also be topped off with a sprinkle of sunflower, chia, pumpkin, hemp, or flax seeds. Avocado is a good fat to include in milkshakes along with a tablespoon of nut butter or coconut oil. These modern milkshakes may contain herbal supplements, yogurt, or raw vegan protein powders. Milkshake connoisseurs might include gourmet ingredients like Madagascar vanilla, fresh vanilla beans, raw cacao powder, tiny farmer's market strawberries, rosewater, manuka honey, and culinary extracts, herbs, and spices.

Healthy sweeteners can be used, including dates, stevia, honey, or maple syrup. Sometimes the fresh fruit alone provides enough sweetness. If the frozen fruits don't make the milkshake thick enough for you, blend in a pile of ice to create a thick, cold, and frothy milkshake.

With all these ideas and ingredients being used, the modern milkshake is born.

Green Milkshakes

For added nutrients, a handful of dark leafy greens may be added to any milkshake. These greens will not change the taste but will make the shake a light green color. Although you may add a handful or two of dark leafy greens or other vegetables to any milkshake recipe, milkshakes should not replace juicing or blended green drinks. However by adding greens to your milkshake you are improving its healthful qualities.

Milkshake smoothies are delicious and decadent. They can be a healthy and, for the most part, a guilt-free treat. For those with candida, diabetes, or hypoglycemia, sugars in any form should be limited. Adjust sweeteners or sweet fruits if you have these conditions.

BASIC MILKSHAKE

This drink is better tasting and healthier than cows' milk.

INGREDIENTS

2 cups almond or cashew milk (see page 185)

½ vanilla bean, seeds scraped from pod

3 Medjool dates or 1 tablespoon maple syrup, coconut nectar, or honey

DIRECTIONS

Blend all ingredients, adding ice if desired. Pour into frosted glass and enjoy.

VERY DECADENT DARK CACAO MILKSHAKE

A dangerously delicious drink you'll be happy you consumed. Notice all the healthy ingredients.

INGREDIENTS

1½ cups almond milk (see page 185)

1 teaspoon vanilla extract, vanilla powder, or ½ vanilla bean, seeds scraped from the pod

1 avocado

¼ cup maple syrup or sweetener of choice to taste

¼ cup raw cacao powder or more if you like it richer

Pinch of sea salt

Pinch of cinnamon

Ice if desired

DIRECTIONS

Blend until smooth, using tamper to keep mixture moving. If your blender does not have a tamper, shut it off and scrape down sides with a spatula. Continue blending and scraping until well blended. If using ice, add and blend again. Taste for sweetness and add more if desired. For a thinner drink add more almond milk. Pour into a tall glass and sprinkle with chopped walnuts, pecans, or nuts of choice. Pop in a straw and sip away. For a video, see my Mimi Kirk YouTube channel or search for "Mimi Kirk's Very Decadent Dark Cacao Milkshake" on YouTube.

THE SPOILER

Warm or cooled this is a healthy alternative to coffee.

INGREDIENTS

½ cup coconut meat

1½ cups almond, cashew, or hemp milk

½ vanilla bean

3 Medjool dates, honey, or stevia to taste

Pinch of cinnamon

DIRECTIONS

Blend all ingredients in order listed until smooth.

HAZELNUT CACAO COCONUT CREAM DREAM

Just as the name implies, a creamy dream of a milk-shake with health-promoting superfoods.

INGREDIENTS

1½ cups hazelnut milk (made like the Basic Nut Milk recipes; see pages 185-190)

½ cup coconut meat from a young Thai coconut or ½ cup unsweetened dried coconut flakes

¼ cup cacao powder

1 tablespoon Lucuma powder

½ vanilla bean, seeds scraped from the pod, or ½ teaspoon vanilla extract

3 Medjool dates or sweetener of choice to taste

Pinch of sea salt

DIRECTIONS

Blend all ingredients in order listed until smooth.

BIG CHILL

Antioxidants, vitamin B, C, potassium, and magnesium all wrapped up in a healthy milkshake.

INGREDIENTS

1½ cups almond or hemp seed milk

1 frozen banana

1 cup frozen or fresh berries of choice

Medjool dates to sweeten to taste

DIRECTIONS

Blend all ingredients in order listed until smooth.

MIXED BERRY COBBLER

High in antioxidants, which can prevent disease and promote a healthy body.

INGREDIENTS

½ cup almond, hemp seed, or coconut milk

½ cup blueberries, fresh or frozen

½ cup strawberries, fresh or frozen

½ cup blackberries, fresh or frozen

2–3 Medjool dates

DIRECTIONS

Blend all ingredients in order listed until smooth.

CHAI

A new start to your morning with this comforting, healthy pick-me-up.

INGREDIENTS

1½ cups almond or cashew milk

2 whole cardamom pods or ½ teaspoon
powdered cardamom

2 black peppercorns

1-inch piece cinnamon stick or ¼ teaspoon
powdered cinnamon

¼ teaspoon fennel seeds

3 thin slices ginger, skin removed

Medjool dates, maple syrup, or stevia to taste

DIRECTIONS

Blend all ingredients in order listed until smooth.

PUMPKIN PIE

If you are one of the lucky ones to like pumpkin pie, you'll be happy to have this milkshake and not have to wait for Thanksgiving.

INGREDIENTS

1½ cups nut milk of choice

3 Medjool dates or maple syrup to taste

1 tablespoon of pumpkin spice mix or make your own by mixing together the following spices:

¼ teaspoon ground cinnamon

¼ teaspoon ground ginger

¼ teaspoon ground cardamom

⅛ teaspoon ground cloves

⅛ teaspoon ground nutmeg

DIRECTIONS

Blend all ingredients in order listed until smooth.

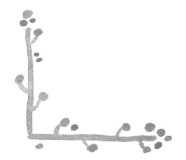

KEY LIME PIE

Limes are known to help cystitis, and keeps your skin looking beautiful. This delicious milkshake can even lower your cholesterol.

INGREDIENTS

1½ cups coconut water

¼ cup coconut meat

Juice from 2–3 limes

1 avocado

1 tablespoon coconut oil

5 Medjool dates

1 dash maple syrup

DIRECTIONS

Blend all ingredients in order listed until smooth.

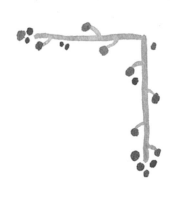

APPLE PIE

Remember apple pie? Well now you can sip on this milkshake without any guilt. Apples, nut milk, and cinnamon, oh my!

INGREDIENTS

1 cup nut or seed milk

2 Fuji apples

1 tablespoon of apple pie spice mix or make your own by mixing together:

¼ teaspoon ground cinnamon

¼ teaspoon ground ginger

¼ ground allspice

⅛ teaspoon ground cloves

⅛ teaspoon fresh or ground nutmeg

DIRECTIONS

Blend all ingredients in order listed until smooth.

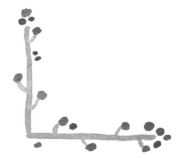

BANANA CREAM PIE

Who would have suspected banana cream pie would be healthy? Well, sip away with a smile on your face because all the ingredients in this milkshake are giving your body some love.

INGREDIENTS

1½ cups nut milk, coconut milk, or
coconut water

½ cup Thai coconut meat

2 frozen bananas

4 Medjool dates

1 teaspoon vanilla extract

Pinch of cinnamon

Dried unsweetened coconut flakes,
sprinkled on top

DIRECTIONS

Blend all ingredients except coconut flakes. Pour into glass and sprinkle top with coconut flakes.

ABC MILKSHAKE

High antioxidants, bone building, and delicious, and all wrapped up in this one little milkshake.

INGREDIENTS

1½ cups nut milk, coconut milk, or
coconut water

1 apple

1 apricot

½ cup frozen blueberries

½ cup frozen cherries

Sweetener if desired

DIRECTIONS

Blend all ingredients in order listed until smooth.

CARROT CAKE

Enhance your eyes, which is an added bonus from the nutrients, while enjoying this carrot cake milkshake.

INGREDIENTS

1 cup pecan milk (made like the Basic Nut Milk recipes; see page 185)

3 carrots juiced or cut into pieces

1 teaspoon vanilla extract

½ frozen banana

¼ teaspoon cinnamon

¼ cup raisins or 2 Medjool dates

DIRECTIONS

Blend all ingredients in order listed until smooth.

CRANBERRY PLEASER

Cranberries have medicinal properties that protect the urinary tract from infection and help cure inflammatory diseases. This creamy pleaser will have you coming back for more.

INGREDIENTS

2 cups coconut water, green tea, or purified water

1 cup fresh cranberries

1 small handful cashews

¼ cup hemp hearts

½ frozen banana

3 Medjool dates

DIRECTIONS

Blend all ingredients in order listed until smooth.

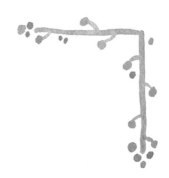

COCONUT, COCONUT

Naturally cooling and electrolyte building in a creamy base of potassium-rich banana, this drink will have you thinking you are on a beautiful island.

INGREDIENTS

1 young Thai coconut, water and meat

½ frozen banana

1 teaspoon vanilla extract or ½ vanilla bean

3 Medjool dates

Pinch of cinnamon or cardamom

Add nut milk if more liquid is needed

DIRECTIONS

Blend all ingredients until smooth. Top with a sprinkle of dried unsweetened coconut flakes.

HYDRATING GREEN MINT CACAO CHIP

If you enjoy chocolate and mint together, this anti-inflammatory, hydrating milkshake will end up being one of your favorites.

INGREDIENTS

1 cup nut milk

1 frozen banana

1 handful mint leaves or ¼ teaspoon mint extract

1 small handful cacao nibs

Pinch of spirulina powder

DIRECTIONS

Blend all ingredients in order listed until smooth.

SIMPLY BLUE

Powerful blueberries high in antioxidants and anti-inflammatory properties all blended up into creamy nut milk will give your body a special healthy treat.

INGREDIENTS

1½ cups nut milk

½ cups young Thai coconut meat or ½ cup dried unsweetened coconut flakes

1 cup frozen blueberries

½ apple

2–3 Medjool dates

DIRECTIONS

Blend all ingredients in order listed until smooth.

STRAWBERRY FIELDS

Sweet strawberries bring summer into your imagination, and just picked ones in season are even better. This delicious milkshake has all the sweet antioxidants you will need to add to your daily healthy intake of nutrients.

INGREDIENTS

1½ cups young Thai coconut water, nut milk, or combination of both

1 cup frozen strawberries

¼ cup pineapple

½ lime, juiced

3 mint sprigs

½ teaspoon vanilla extract

DIRECTIONS

Blend all ingredients in order listed until smooth.

PEACH MILKSHAKE

This milkshake is a delicious summer treat and at the same time adds a good portion of your daily-required fruit intake.

INGREDIENTS

1 cup almond or hemp seed milk

1 cup fresh or frozen peaches

½ cup fresh pineapple juice

½ frozen banana

1 teaspoon coconut oil

DIRECTIONS

Blend all ingredients in order listed until smooth.

HEMP SEED DELIGHT

A powerful protein-rich creamy milkshake, which is high in potassium and vitamins, will help with detoxifying and building bone strength.

INGREDIENTS

3 tablespoons shelled hemp seed

1½ cups filtered water

½ frozen banana

1 tablespoon tahini

Pinch of cinnamon

½ teaspoon vanilla or ½ vanilla bean

1 handful dark leafy greens

2–3 Medjool dates or sweetener of choice

DIRECTIONS

Blend all ingredients in order listed until smooth.

SIP THIS

Very simple and delicious, this milkshake is potassium rich and heart healthy.

INGREDIENTS

1½ cups almond or cashew milk

¼ cup coconut meat

½ banana, frozen

1 stone fruit in season

Pinch of cinnamon or cardamom

Maple syrup or sweetener of choice to taste

DIRECTIONS

Blend all ingredients in order listed until smooth.

NUT BUTTER MILKSHAKE

This milkshake is a special treat comprised of a deep rich flavor and the power of antioxidants.

INGREDIENTS

1 cup almond milk

2 bananas, frozen

1 tablespoon cacao powder

¼ cup nut butter of choice

1 tablespoon maple syrup

½ teaspoon vanilla extract

Pinch of sea salt

Ice if desired

DIRECTIONS

Blend all ingredients in order listed until smooth.

FRAPPUCCINO

Just in case you've been craving a bit of coffee flavor in a healthy, protein-rich milkshake, well here it is.

INGREDIENTS

3 tablespoons hemp seeds

1 cup filtered water

½ teaspoon vanilla extract

½ teaspoon coffee extract or 3 teaspoons cold-pressed decaffeinated coffee

Sweetener of choice

½ cup ice, more or less if desired

DIRECTIONS

Blend all ingredients in order listed until smooth.

THE COOL GREEN ONE

This healthy milkshake has dark leafy greens added for an extra boost of energy.

INGREDIENTS

1–1½ cups coconut water or coconut milk

⅓ cup pineapple juice

½ banana, frozen

1 handful dark leafy greens

2 basil leaves

DIRECTIONS

Blend all ingredients in order listed until smooth.

JUICING FOR SPECIFIC HEALTH CONDITIONS

Juicing has been known to help strengthen the immune system, eliminate cancer cells, and protect against free radicals.

Juicing is known to help in the quick recovery from many health issues, including some cancers. Drink at least 16 ounces to 32 ounces daily. If you are recovering from an illness, then 32 ounces is recommended. Juicing has been known to help strengthen the immune system, eliminate cancer cells, and protect against free radicals. Juicing is recommended in place of blending when healing from any illness or disease.

It takes approximately 3–6 pounds of vegetables and fruit to make 16 ounces of juice. That's one reason a juice can cost $10 and up at a juice bar.

At the Gerson Therapy Institute in San Diego, a natural approach to heal cancer, arthritis, heart disease, allergies, and many other degenerative diseases is practiced. Patients consume daily between 15–20 pounds of juiced organically grown vegetables. Each patient drinks up to one 8-ounce glass every hour, up to 13 times per day. Watch the Gerson Miracle on their website, Gerson.org.

Refer to page 58 for an A–Z guide to beneficial vegetables and fruits for combating specific diseases and illnesses.

Inflammation is the root cause of many serious illnesses, including heart disease, many cancers, and Alzheimer's.

. . . .

ANTI-INFLAMMATORY JUICE #1

INGREDIENTS

2 celery stalks

2 carrots

2 pears, do not need to remove core when juicing

2 apples

1 lemon

2- to 3-inch piece of fresh turmeric or ½ teaspoon powdered

2-inch piece fresh ginger

DIRECTIONS

Juice all ingredients in the order listed. If using powdered turmeric, vigorously mix into juice with a spoon as the powder settles to the bottom quickly.

ANTI-INFLAMMATORY JUICE #2

INGREDIENTS

1 cucumber

1–2 carrots

1 orange, juiced

1 pear, do not have to remove core when juicing

2 celery stalks

½ bunch romaine lettuce

2- to 3-inch piece fresh turmeric or 1 teaspoon powdered

DIRECTIONS

Juice all ingredients in the order listed. If using powdered turmeric, vigorously mix into juice with a spoon as the powder settles to the bottom quickly.

FOR CANDIDA AND YEAST INFECTION

Probiotics are important to maintain a healthy balance and can be purchased refrigerated or in capsules at a health food store or online. Refrigerated probiotics will assure its aliveness. If you can't locate refrigerated probiotics, purchase capsules. Take them as specified on the label.

A juice cleanse is suggested to clear and prevent candida from reappearing. Three days of juicing, drinking approximately 64 ounces daily, using a combination of any of the following is recommended:

- Kale
- Cabbage
- Cucumbers
- Beets
- Spinach
- Broccoli
- Dandelion root
- Lemons
- Limes
- Garlic

In addition, it's very important to drink 64 ounces of water daily. (See page 290 for infused waters.) To alkaline your water, squeeze the juice of one lemon for every 8 ounces of water. Eat raw vegetables along with juicing if hungry. Be sure to chew very well to break down the particles of food before swallowing.

FOR COLDS

Before buying over-the-counter medication or taking prescription drugs try this natural cold reliever.

A COLD KILLER

INGREDIENTS

1 bunch parsley

2 small garlic cloves

½ beet

1 carrot

2 oranges, juiced

1-inch piece of ginger

Liquid of choice as needed

DIRECTIONS

Blend all ingredients, adding liquid as necessary.

FOR EYES

Taking care of your eyes before any problems arise is a good investment for your future eyesight. Smoking and alcohol can contribute to eye problems, including cataracts, macular degeneration, and other eye diseases.

As we age, eye care is essential. If you have family history of eye disease, you might want to visit an ophthalmologist for an eye exam. If you are age 50+, you should see an eye care professional for a comprehensive dilated eye exam as part of your annual routine health care. He or she can tell you how often you need to have a checkup based on your individual risk factors for eye disease. Learn more about comprehensive dilated eye exams from the National Eye Institute at their website, nei.nih.gov.

Green and orange vegetables are a great source of antioxidants, which are good for eyes. Eyes need lutein and zeaxanthin, vitamins A, C, and E, along with beta-carotene, zinc, and copper to keep them healthy. Fresh dark leafy greens, including kale, spinach, turnip greens, collard greens, dandelion greens, and mustard greens, top the list with 8–25 milligrams of lutein and zeaxanthin per serving.

Don't take your eyes for granted. As we age, more eye issues arise. Juicing helps to support eye health.

EYE JUICE ONE

INGREDIENTS

5 romaine lettuce leaves

3 kale leaves, stems removed

1 handful spinach

2 beet leaves

4 carrots

¼ cup broccoli

DIRECTIONS

Juice all ingredients in order listed. If blending, add liquid as needed.

EYE JUICE TWO

INGREDIENTS

1 handful collard, mustard, or spinach greens

½ papaya

1 kiwi, cut in half and fruit scooped out

¼ piece red bell pepper

2 tablespoons hemp seeds or sunflower seeds

½ orange or 1 whole tangerine, juiced

6 parsley sprigs

6 strawberries

DIRECTIONS

Juice all ingredients in order listed. If blending, add liquid as needed.

FOR HEADACHES

If you are prone to headaches, this juice can help relieve them. It's easy to pop a pill, but if you are trying to improve your health, there is nothing like a natural cure.

HEADACHE JUICE

INGREDIENTS

1 cucumber

2 apples

6 kale leaves, stems removed

3 celery stalks

½ lemon, juiced

1-inch piece ginger or 1 garlic clove

DIRECTIONS

Juice all ingredients in order listed. If blending, add liquid as needed.

FOR INSOMNIA AND OTHER SLEEP DISORDERS

Being deprived of sleep can affect your health. Snoring, insomnia, sleep apnea, and restless leg syndrome are all common sleep disorders. Going to sleep too late and getting up too early can encourage heart disease, strokes, and high blood pressure. Poor sleep is associated with the inability to concentrate. Sleeping pills and sedatives can only add to health problems. Using a natural approach to correct the problems of sleep deprivation should be our first choice. Juicing certain vegetables and fruits during the day can help to change your constitution and in turn help you sleep better. The following is a list of vegetables and fruits that can help you sleep by relaxing muscle and internal organs: spinach, kale, chard, parsley, broccoli, cucumbers, kiwi, strawberries, bananas, apricots, sour cherries, tomatoes, mint, pomegranate, red grapes, and concord grapes.

In addition to juicing, remove all electronic devices from your bedroom before going to sleep and create a ritual before going to bed. Take a warm bath, try wearing pajamas or some clothing to bed that you don't wear outside, don't eat anything two hours before going to bed, and shut off the television and computer at least ½ to 1 hour before trying to sleep.

TO SLEEP TIGHT

We need to get our eight hours of beauty sleep every night, nine if you're ugly. —Betty White

INGREDIENTS

3 stalks celery

1 cabbage leaf

¼ cucumber, no need to peel if it's organic

½ banana

DIRECTIONS

Juice all ingredients in order listed. If blending, add liquid as needed.

FOR INTESTINAL AND DIGESTIVE DISORDERS

Our gut health is paramount for living a long healthy life, and we must do everything we can to keep our cells and digestive tract healthy. Any intestinal issues should get your attention, including bloating, gas, and acid reflux. Juicing the right vegetables and fruits can make a positive difference. Let your health professional know your symptoms as well.

DIGESTION JUICE

INGREDIENTS

1 lemon, juiced

5 carrots

½ small beet

½ sweet red bell pepper

1–2 pinches of cayenne pepper to taste

DIRECTIONS

Juice all ingredients in order listed. If blending, add liquid as needed.

INTESTINE HEALTH JUICE

INGREDIENTS

½ medium cucumber

5 cilantro sprigs

3 kale leaves, stems removed

½ cup broccoli

1-inch piece ginger

1 Granny Smith (green) apple

DIRECTIONS

Juice all ingredients in order listed. If blending, add liquid as needed.

FOR KIDNEY IMPORTANCE

The kidneys' main job is to filter the waste out of the blood. For our body to work properly, it must have water. Our kidneys regulate water by removing excess water or retaining water when the body needs it. Kidneys also excrete excess minerals, such as sodium and potassium, through the urine. Our kidneys regulate calcium and phosphate levels. Many waste products are toxic to our body, and a healthy, functioning kidney decreases these toxins. Our kidneys produce and make important hormones, which circulate in the bloodstream and regulate blood pressure. Be good to your kidneys and they will be good to you.

KIDNEY HEALTH JUICE #1

Not to exceed 8 ounces daily. Best to drink a small amount 2 or3 times daily.

INGREDIENTS

8 asparagus stalks

2 stalks celery

DIRECTIONS

Juice ingredients together.

KIDNEY HEALTH JUICE #2

This juice is recommended for kidney, liver, bladder, and pancreatic cancers.

INGREDIENTS

1 bunch parsley or cilantro

½ cucumber

1 celery stalk

1 kale leaf, stem removed

1 apple

½ lemon, juiced

DIRECTIONS

Juice all ingredients in order listed. If blending, add liquid as needed.

KIDNEY HEALTH JUICE #3

INGREDIENTS

1 cup watermelon

2 parsley sprigs

2 nettle leaves

2 dandelion leaves

Liquid as needed

DIRECTIONS

Juice all ingredients in order listed. If blending, add liquid as needed.

FOR LOVING YOUR LIVER

Don't ignore or abuse your liver as it's the largest organ in your body, after skin, and serves an important purpose. Our liver makes bile to help break down food, remove toxic chemicals, and build muscle, just to name a few benefits. When we don't take care of our liver, we can become very ill and our liver may become swollen and diseased. When we eat healthy and refrain from smoking, drinking alcohol, or using medication or drugs, we can keep our liver healthy. Juicing can help reverse an unhealthy liver or help to maintain a healthy one.

LIVER HEALTH JUICE #1

INGREDIENTS

1 grapefruit, juiced

1 apple

½ cup cabbage

½ lemon, juiced

2 celery ribs

4 romaine lettuce leaves

1-inch piece ginger, peeled

Handful of parsley

1-inch piece turmeric

DIRECTIONS

Juice all ingredients together. If blending, add liquid as needed.

LIVER HEALTH JUICE #2

INGREDIENTS

½ beet

1 apple

4 parsley sprigs

1-inch piece ginger

2-inch piece turmeric

2-inch piece aloe vera (see page 71)

DIRECTIONS

Juice all ingredients. If blending, add liquid as needed. If using powdered turmeric, stir directly into glass.

FOR LUNGS

Reactions to chemicals in the air can irritate lungs. Try this potent juice to relieve irritation.

LUNG HEALTH JUICE

INGREDIENTS

1-inch slice of daikon with skin on

1–2 ripe pears

1½-inch piece of lotus root with skin on

DIRECTIONS

Juice all ingredients in order listed and drink immediately.

FOR OVERALL HEALTH

Maintaining one's health is a practical goal. As we age, our bodies can weaken if we do not support it with the right nutrients. Drinking the following juice will provide your body with some needed vitamins and nutrients.

OVERALL HEALTH JUICE

INGREDIENTS

1 medium beet

1 large carrot

1 green or Fuji apple

DIRECTIONS

Juice all ingredients in order listed.

FOR TUMORS OR PANCREAS

Preventive medicine through proper nutrition may be the answer to a long healthy life. Keeping our bodies' inner workings healthy with the proper vegetables and fruits will aid in this effort.

TUMOR OR PANCREAS HEALTH JUICE ONE

INGREDIENTS

1 Granny Smith (green) apple

½ cucumber

3 medium asparagus

2 carrots

1-inch piece ginger

DIRECTIONS

Juice all ingredients in order listed and drink immediately.

TUMOR OR PANCREAS HEALTH JUICE TWO

INGREDIENTS

¼ cup daikon radish

1 carrot

1 Granny Smith (green) apple

½ cucumber

½ beet

1-inch piece ginger

DIRECTIONS

Juice all ingredients in order listed and drink immediately.

TUMOR OR PANCREAS HEALTH JUICE THREE

INGREDIENTS

1 cucumber

1 cup spinach

2 carrots

½ beet

1 Granny Smith (green) apple

DIRECTIONS

Juice all ingredients in order listed and drink immediately.

FOR WEIGHT LOSS

Diets don't work for most people. We lose weight and gain
it back again and for some people it's a lifelong challenge.
Juice is known to help reduce unwanted weight and provide nutrients that keep our bodies satiated and away from
making unhealthy choices.

WEIGHT LOSS JUICE

INGREDIENTS

1 orange, juiced

½ medium beet

2 celery stalks

1 handful spinach

½ lemon, juiced

1-inch piece ginger

DIRECTIONS

Juice all ingredients in order listed.

Shots and Boosts

Shots and boosts are supplements to juicing or blending. They can be made and added to a juice, or consumed straight on their own. They are quick pick-me-ups instead of coffee or other stimulants. Supplements used should be in liquid form. For recipes with a citrus ingredient, either peel citrus and put segments through juicer or juice separately and stir into finished drink.

For maximum strength, juicing shots and boosts is recommended as opposed to blending, where water must be added, which dilutes the drink. Drink immediately for cell rejuvenation.

ALKALINE BOOST

An alkaline body is important in order to maintain healthy organs, digestion, and skin. Keeping your body more alkaline may prevent common diseases and helps to repair the body from injury.

INGREDIENTS

½ cucumber

1 celery stalk

4 parsley sprigs

1-inch piece ginger

½ lime, juiced

¼ avocado

DIRECTIONS

Juice all ingredients in order listed except avocado. Place juice in blender and add avocado.

ANTIOXIDANT SHOT

Antioxidants can minimize damage to cells from free radicals and help your body protect itself from the rigors of oxidation.

INGREDIENTS

3–4 ounces of pomegranate, gogi berry, and/or cranberry juice

Dash of honey to sweeten, if desired

DIRECTIONS

Juice one or all together. Soak 1 handful of gogi berries in 4 ounces of water to soften. Let marinate 2 hours or overnight. Blend water and berries together. For cranberries, juice berries adding water and/or lemon. Stir in a dash of honey to juiced fruit to sweeten. Pomegranate seeds may be juiced and consumed straight, without added water.

B VITAMIN SHOT

Vitamin B is important for a healthy body as it helps us to think clearly and generate new healthy cells. Vitamin B deficiency can cause signs of early aging.

INGREDIENTS

1 dropper of B12 complex liquid vitamin

½ cup lemon water

1–2 oranges, juiced

DIRECTIONS

Mix all ingredients together in a glass and drink.

CALCIUM BOOST

Calcium is important for our overall health. Almost every cell in our body uses calcium in some way. Calcium affects our nervous system, muscles, heart, and bones.

It's best to get your calcium needs from natural healthy food sources.

INGREDIENTS

2 kale leaves, stems removed

1 beet or turnip greens

1 small broccoli floret

½ celery stalk

2 apples

2 carrots

DIRECTIONS

Juice all ingredients.

BLOOD SHOT

Keep your blood healthy as it does its job to transport nutrients throughout your body. Blood is also used to remove waste products from the body, such as carbon dioxide.

INGREDIENTS

½ cucumber

½ lime, juiced

¼ small beet

DIRECTIONS

Juice all ingredients.

ENERGY SHOT

You can count on this shot to boost your energy in a healthy way instead of commercial energy drinks that spike your metabolism and play havoc with your health.

INGREDIENTS

2–3 ounces water

2 drops ginseng

2 drops vitamin E

1 teaspoon honey

DIRECTIONS

Stir together all ingredients.

CHLOROPHYLL BOOST

Chlorophyll has been shown to increase oxygen uptake in the blood, which increases energy and improves blood disorders. Chlorophyll has anticarcinogenic properties and supplies our bodies with micronutrients and magnesium, which is how our body produces energy.

INGREDIENTS

½ cup spinach

3 romaine leaves

1 tablespoon blue-green algae

1 Granny Smith (green) apple

¼ bunch of parsley

DIRECTIONS

Juice all ingredients in order listed.

GALLBLADDER BOOST

Many doctors tell you that you don't need your gall-bladder and if it gets infected, they immediately want to remove it. Keep your gallbladder healthy because your liver produces bile, which emulsifies fats to improve your fat digestion. The gallbladder stores half of this emulsified fat until it's needed. Stay healthy and keep your gallbladder; it serves a purpose.

INGREDIENTS

1 grapefruit, juiced

1-inch piece ginger

¼ cup mint leaves

½ cup pineapple

DIRECTIONS

Juice all ingredients in order listed.

FLU SHOT

Having the flu can get you down, but before you run out to get some over-the-counter drugs, try this Flu Shot to boost your immunity.

INGREDIENTS

1 large lemon, juiced

7 cilantro sprigs

1-inch piece of ginger

Honey to taste, if desired

DIRECTIONS

Juice all ingredients, except honey. Stir in honey. Warm up if desired.

GALLSTONE BOOST

Gallstones can be very painful. People who consume sugars and dietary fats are more likely to have gallstones. Excess cholesterol may form into crystals and eventually into stones. A heart-healthy diet can help prevent stones.

INGREDIENTS

1 apple, cored

½ lemon, juiced

1 lime, juiced

1-inch piece parsnip

1 pear

1 radish

DIRECTIONS

Juice all ingredients in order listed.

GINGER SHOT

Ginger relieves gastrointestinal disorders and nausea. Ginger is good for inflammatory diseases and a healthy immune system.

INGREDIENTS

2-inch piece of ginger

½ lemon, juiced

1 orange, juiced

DIRECTIONS

Juice all ingredients together.

HORMONE BOOST

Maca is used to balance hormones in both women and men. Maca helps with mood swings, depression, cramps, and hot flashes.

INGREDIENTS

1 teaspoon maca powder

½ cup cooled green tea

Juice from ½ apple

½ lemon, juiced

Honey to taste

DIRECTIONS

Mix or blend all ingredients together in the order listed.

IMMUNITY SHOT

The key to good health is a strong immune system. It can combat pollution, allergens, poor diet, stress, and aging.

INGREDIENTS

1 large lemon, juiced

1-inch piece of ginger

½ apple

Pinch of cayenne

2 drops oregano oil

DIRECTIONS

Juice lemon, ginger, and apple, and stir in cayenne and oregano oil.

METABOLISM BOOST

Our body needs energy, which is provided through our metabolism. We are constantly burning calories to keep our bodies going, but if we eat a very low calorie diet, our body thinks it's starving, and to survive it will slow down our metabolism and not burn fat.

INGREDIENTS

½ grapefruit, juiced

½ cup blueberries

½ cup cooled green tea

DIRECTIONS

Juice grapefruit. Pour into blender with blueberries and green tea. Blend until smooth.

OMEGA 3 SHOT

High in omega-3 fatty acids and packed with protein and fiber, chia seeds can boost energy, lower cholesterol, aid in digestion, support stronger teeth and bones, improve heart health, and stabilize blood sugar.

INGREDIENTS

3 ounces cooled green tea

1 teaspoon chia seeds

DIRECTIONS

Stir chia seeds into cooled green tea. The longer it sits, the thicker it gets; so drink within 5 minutes.

POMEGRANATE SHOT

The most powerful antioxidants of all fruits, pomegranate is known to remove atherosclerotic plaque, lower blood pressure, and reduce heart attacks and strokes.

Pomegranate juice may also be added to smoothies, juices, and milkshakes. The white inner seed will leave a little grit, which can be strained out. Pomegranate juice found at supermarkets are processed, but if you purchase some look for 100 percent pure pomegranate juice.

INGREDIENTS

1 pomegranate, seeded (see page 63)

DIRECTIONS

Juice seeds and drink immediately.

REJUVENATION BOOST

Need a quick rejuvenation boost? Bee pollen is an energy enhancer and immune system builder, and it supports the cardiovascular system. Buy local pollen granules directly from beekeeper or from reliable sources.

INGREDIENTS

1 tablespoon bee pollen granules

DIRECTIONS

Add granules to juice or tea water.

SKIN BOOST

An adult body is 50-75 percent water. Staying hydrated is important for ultimate health and can keep your skin glowing. Drink 8 glasses of water daily and for a quick skin boost, drink the following.

INGREDIENTS

1 lemon, juiced

½ green apple

½ cucumber

DIRECTIONS

Juice all ingredients in order listed.

MANGOSTEEN SHOT

Provides powerful support for every organ in the human body. Combats inflammation and cancer. The inside of a mangosteen looks like a tangerine with several segments. Most segments have a seed inside, either soft or hard and in varying sizes. The shell, which has many healing properties, can be juiced, but only a very small piece as it can be tart.

INGREDIENTS

2-3 mangosteens

DIRECTIONS

Juice, or if blended add ½ cup of coconut water.

WHEATGRASS CHLOROPHYLL BOOST

Wheatgrass is a powerful detoxifier. It stimulates the thyroid gland, contains beneficial enzymes, and restores alkalinity to the blood. There are even claims that it turns gray hair to its natural color again.

INGREDIENTS

1 Granny Smith (green) apple

½ cup of wheatgrass (approximately 2–3 handfuls), or 1-ounce shot of wheatgrass

½ lemon, juiced

1-inch piece of ginger

1 teaspoon blue-green algae, spirulina, or green powder of choice

DIRECTIONS

Juice apple and wheatgrass and mix or blend in balance of ingredients. If your juicer is not good at juicing wheatgrass, wrap the wheatgrass in a lettuce leaf and run through juicer.

WHEATGRASS SHOT

Wheatgrass should be cut fresh and juiced. A slow auger juicer works best. If your juicer is not good at juicing wheatgrass, wrap the wheatgrass in a lettuce leaf and run through juicer.

INGREDIENTS

½ cup of wheatgrass (approximately 2–3 handfuls), or 1-ounce shot of wheatgrass

1-inch piece ginger

1 orange wedge chaser

DIRECTIONS

Juice wheatgrass and ginger. Drink the shot and chase with the orange wedge.

Good Food Sources to Fight Diseases

What Ails You?

· · · · · · · · · · · · · · · · · · ·

The following information does not constitute the practice of medicine and does not replace the advice of your physician or other health care provider. Before undertaking any course of treatment, be sure to check with your physician or health care provider.

GLOSSARY FROM A–Z

The A–Z glossary is a tool to learn what foods are good for a specific illness or disease. Each ailment lists foods that are known to help heal and repair that particular ailment or disease. You may juice any one or a combination of any of the listed vegetables or fruits in the category that apply to your condition. Add any of these items daily to existing juice or blender recipes, or juice and consume any single ingredient on its own. Organic only please!

Acid Reflux—apples, stone fruits (including peaches, plums, and nectarines), bananas, melons, berries, romaine lettuce, sweet bell peppers, celery, and zucchini

Acne—carrots, romaine lettuce, spinach, beets, papaya, strawberries, cucumbers, grapes, apricots, and green peppers

Aging—apples, blueberries, figs, grapes, grapefruit, watermelon, cantaloupe, oranges, papaya, pears, raspberries, strawberries, beets, broccoli, cabbage, carrots, celery, leafy greens, onions, pumpkin, sweet potatoes, and tomatoes

Allergies, Seasonal—carrots, celery, beets, cucumber, kiwi, dark leafy greens, berries, stone fruits, and bananas

Anemia—apples, tomatoes, bananas, lemons, oranges, grapes, raisins, figs, bell peppers, spinach, broccoli, green cabbage, beets, celery, kale, almonds, dates, and walnuts

Arterial Plaque—garlic, ginger, red grapes, concord grapes, blueberries, blackberries, strawberries, raspberries, apples, spinach, olive oil, tomatoes, green tea, pomegranate, kiwi, cantaloupe, cherries, grapefruit, sweet potatoes, chard, and flaxseeds

Arthritis—apples, beets, carrots, celery, watermelon, cucumber, blueberries, strawberries, raspberries, pomegranate, spinach, parsley, watercress, kale, pineapple, papaya, ginger, romaine lettuce, plums, cherries, and grapes

Back Pain—all dark leafy greens, watermelon, grapes, ginger, cherries, pomegranate, apples, carrots, celery, cucumbers, turmeric, and ginger

Bad Breath—apples, parsley, ginger, mint, dark leafy greens, alfalfa sprouts, cucumbers

Belly Fat—blueberries, watermelon, cherries, young Thai coconut meat, coconut oil, coconut milk or water, avocados, tomatoes, pears, apples, celery, grapefruit, sweet peppers, bananas, and pomegranates

Bladder—carrots, celery, peas, carrots, cabbage, spinach, parsley, cucumbers, beets, cranberries, melons, and pears

Bronchitis—garlic, ginger, carrots, spinach, radishes, celery, beets, cucumbers, oranges, pineapple, peaches, lemons, pears, and peppermint

Bloating—bananas, ginger, asparagus, dark leafy greens, Granny Smith (green apple) red apples, berries, grapefruit, lemons, limes, peppermint (avoid eating cruciferous vegetables and combining starches and fruits if you experience bloating—see food combining page 55)

Blood Pressure—bananas, carrots, cucumbers, parsley, spinach, celery, beets, sunflower seeds, pumpkin seeds, avocados, cacao, grapes, oranges, broccoli, cantaloupe, winter squash, and turmeric

Bone Health—dark leafy greens, spinach, collard greens, oranges, escarole, figs, sesame seeds, beet greens, kale, cabbage, and broccoli

Cancer—carrots, celery, spinach, cabbage, apples, tomatoes, watermelon, grapefruit, grapes, papaya, wheatgrass, berries, sweet potatoes, ground flaxseed, turmeric, pomegranates, broccoli, cauliflower, and brussels sprouts

Celiac—broccoli, collards, all dark leafy greens, fruits, berries, and vegetables (no gluten whatsoever—all vegetables and fruits are free of gluten including nuts and seeds)

Cholesterol—cabbage, blueberries, grapes, avocados, carrots, tomatoes, walnuts, almonds, pistachios, and oranges

Colds—carrots, celery, lemons, oranges, and grapefruit

Colitis—napa or savoy cabbage (if using a blender, strain the juices), carrots, apples, and a small piece of beet

Constipation—carrots, apples, celery, spinach, grapes, prunes, dates, and berries

Crohn's—all dark leafy greens, sweet red bell peppers, bananas, flaxseed oil, and coconut oil

Dementia—beets, dark leafy greens, celery, cabbage, and apples

Diabetes—brussels sprouts, spinach, lettuce, cabbage, broccoli, carrots, radishes, and celery

Diarrhea—carrots, apples, celery, spinach, parsley, raspberries, and blackberries

Edema—berries, tomatoes, cherries, watermelon, parsley, cabbage, beets, grapes, dark leafy greens, pumpkin, leaks, pineapple, and asparagus

Eyes—broccoli, peas, brussels sprouts, green beans, summer and winter squash, beet greens, pumpkin, romaine

lettuce, asparagus, carrots, spinach, celery, parsley, apples, kiwis, blackberries, pears, grapes, and cranberries

Fatigue—dark leafy greens, parsley, limes, mangoes, bananas, pineapple, broccoli, carrots, strawberries, ginger, cinnamon, garlic, and peppermint

Fibroid Tumors—broccoli, cabbage, brussels sprouts, cucumbers, carrots, asparagus, ginger, turmeric, daikon radish, green apple, spinach, and beets

Fibromyalgia—carrots, celery, parsley, spinach, lettuce, cucumbers, lemons, and ginger

Gallbladder—beets, cucumbers, tomatoes, apples, grapes, avocados, flaxseed, sweet potatoes (not yams), chard, dandelion, lettuce (but not bitter), celery, and carrots

Gallstones—Granny Smith (green) apples, beets, radishes, and cherries

GI Tract—kale, cucumbers, spinach, ginger, bananas, and asparagus

Gout—apples, grapes, cherries, lemons, limes, pineapple, and strawberries

Headache—carrots, spinach, celery, parsley, beets, cucumbers, and lettuce

Heart—carrots, spinach, celery, parsley, cucumbers, oranges, guavas, papaya, and avocados

Hepatitis—eat more fruits and vegetables, including carrots, beets, parsley, cucumbers, dandelion, radishes, dark leafy greens, squash, berries, and cherries

High Blood Pressure—see Hypertension

Hormone—beets, broccoli, carrots, grapefruit, tomatoes, ginger, maca, dark leafy greens, berries, and sweet bell peppers

Hyperactivity—leeks, kale, mustard greens, collard greens, beet greens, peas, broccoli, kale, sunflower seeds, walnuts, flax, hemp and chia seeds, avocado, spinach, celery, oranges, bananas, and dark leafy greens

Hypertension—apples, apricots, fennel, cabbage, pears, strawberries, grapefruit, lemons, oranges, carrots, cucumbers, parsley, spinach, celery, dark leafy greens, beets, bananas, sunflower seeds, raw cacao, dates, and watermelon

Hypothyroidism—see Thyroid

Immune—oranges, grapefruit, strawberries, kiwi, cantaloupes, broccoli, spinach, carrots, bell peppers, cauliflower, and sweet potatoes

Inflammation—radishes, pineapple, ginger, avocado, garlic, turmeric, asparagus, kale, chard, broccoli, brussels sprouts, cabbage, cauliflower, spinach, tomatoes, dark salad greens, carrots, berries, pomegranates, and apples

Insomnia—carrots, spinach, celery, lettuce, sour cherries, ginger, tomatoes, mint, broccoli, pomegranate, bananas, brussels sprouts, cucumbers, red grapes, concord grapes, red grapes, strawberries, and pineapple

Irritable Bowel Syndrome (IBS)—apples, apricots, kiwi, lemons, papaya, pineapple, carrots, parsley, spinach, tomatoes, lettuce, celery, beets, cabbage, and broccoli

Joint pain—dark cherry juice, parsley, broccoli, spinach, carrots, ginger, pineapple, apples, and turmeric

Juvenile arthritis—blueberries, strawberries, raspberries, spinach, cauliflower, cabbage, red peppers, broccoli, oranges, grapefruits, pomegranates, and cranberries

Kidney—parsley, cranberries, lemons, carrots, dandelion, celery, cucumbers, papaya, sprouts, watermelon, spirulina or blue-green algae, grapes, blueberries, fennel beets, spinach, string beans, asparagus, apples, pears, zucchini, and bell peppers

Leukemia—(all organic only) blueberries, tomatoes, cherries, kale, spinach, bell peppers, gogi berries, cauliflower, broccoli, Brussels sprouts, cabbage, kale, yams, carrots, kale, spinach, collards, flaxseeds, and all dark leafy greens

Liver—carrots, lemons, beets, parsley, cucumbers, dandelion, radishes, ginger, garlic, celery, daikon radish, flax oil or seeds, apples, cabbage, cinnamon, and turmeric

Lupus—Avoid high protein foods, soy products, and alfalfa sprouts. Eat all organic dark leafy greens, berries, apricots, sweet potatoes, aloe vera, carrots, cinnamon, ginger, garlic, nuts, and seeds.

Menstrual Cramps/PMS—dill, sesame seeds, parsley, celery, cacao, spinach, chard, broccoli, summer squash, all dark leafy greens, cabbage, cauliflower, artichokes, peas, avocados, apples, raspberries, pears, strawberries, boysenberries, grapefruit, apricots, flaxseed, and sunflower seeds

Migraine Headache—carrots, spinach, celery, parsley, sweet potatoes, chard, sunflower seeds, watermelon, sesame seeds, almonds, and flaxseeds

Mucus—carrots, apples, pineapple, celery, beets, cucumbers, garlic, watercress, parsley, lemons, all berries, grapefruit, orange, tomatoes, dark leafy greens, broccoli, brussels sprouts, bell peppers, cucumbers, kale, jicama, olives, sea vegetables, tomatoes, and zucchini

Nausea—apples, ginger, nuts, bananas, mint, watermelon, lemons, ginger, cantaloupe, carrots, celery, grapes, apples, pears, and peaches

Obesity—more vegetables and fruits, cut out or eat less meat, dairy, starches, and processed foods (also see Weight Control)

Osteopenia/Osteoporosis—broccoli, collard greens, bok choy, kale, romaine lettuce, spinach, sweet potatoes, turnip greens, oranges, sesame seeds, cucumbers, and celery

Pancreas—blueberries, cherries, red or black grapes, broccoli, brussels sprouts, garlic, spinach, sweet potatoes, tomatoes, dark leafy greens, sea vegetables, bell peppers, squash, and lots of water

Psoriasis—Omit foods that cause inflammation, including meat, eggs, butter, white flour, dairy, and gluten. A well-balanced diet of organic fresh fruits and vegetables is recommended. Juice and eat high antioxidant and vitamin rich foods, such as berries, parsley, oranges, beets, kale, spinach, lettuce, cucumbers, celery, peaches, apples, cherries, apricots, asparagus, broccoli, cabbage, cauliflower, brussels sprouts, zucchini, and kale.

Rheumatism—carrots, celery, spinach, parsley, lettuce, watercress, and cucumbers

Rosacea—Omit cigarettes and acidic foods, including meat, dairy, coffee, sugars, alcohol, and sodas. Consume alkaline foods including brussels sprouts, cabbage, cauliflower, celery, cucumbers, parsley, kale, spinach, lettuce, sprouts, peas, zucchini, avocados, tomatoes, almonds, Brazil nuts, pumpkin, sunflower, and sesame seeds, garlic, lemons, and limes.

Sinus—carrots, spinach, beets, and cucumbers

Skin—pineapple, cantaloupe, watermelon, cucumbers, bananas, brussels sprouts, red grapes, and concord grapes

Teeth and Gums—carrots, pears, celery, cucumbers, beets, watercress, strawberries, apples, watermelon, bananas, pineapple, oranges, and garlic

Thyroid/Hypothyroidism—bananas, prunes, flaxseeds, seaweed (arame, kelp, dulse, hijike, nori, wakame, kombu), coconut oil, radishes, celery, parsley, blueberries, blackberries, raspberries, apples, avocados, mushrooms, pumpkin, green peas, bell peppers, sweet potatoes, dates, raisins, apricots, and zucchini

Toxemia/Preeclampsia—carrots, parsley, celery, spinach, cucumbers, apples, kale, cabbage, broccoli, cantaloupes, kiwi, tomatoes, citrus fruits, seeds, nuts, and raisins

Ulcer—cabbage, celery, broccoli, melons, papaya, pears, peaches, berries, apples, bell peppers, pineapple, and ginger

Urinary Tract Infection—blueberries, cranberries, watermelon, lemons, celery, fennel, carrots, parsnip, cumin, garlic, nettle, garlic, radishes, and ginger

Vaginitis—spinach, kale, broccoli, sea vegetables, almonds, bell peppers, cherries, tomatoes, sweet potatoes, lemons, limes, grapefruit, oranges, sprouts, cucumbers, sunflower seeds, and garlic

Vitiligo—Oranges, grapefruit, lemons, dark leafy greens, beets, carrots, tomatoes, green peppers, asparagus, spinach, green peas, broccoli, crimini and shiitake mushrooms, turnip greens, black strap molasses, sesame seeds, almonds, walnuts, cashews, sunflower seeds, pumpkin seeds, sweet potatoes. Enjoy foods rich in vitamin B12, omega-3 fatty acid; avoid blueberries and pears.

Weight Control—All fruits and vegetables are good for weight control. Forgo processed foods, white flour, sugar, and sodas. Juice and eat dark leafy greens, broccoli, celery, cucumbers, carrots, fennel, daikon, bell peppers, apples, bananas, pears, oranges, plums, kiwis, grapefruits, pineapple, melons, apricots, grapes, cherries, and berries.

Wrinkles—watercress, blueberries, raspberries, cucumbers, cantaloupe, coconut, coconut oil, olive oil, olives, turmeric, cacao, avocados, nuts, and seeds

COMPLETE GUIDE TO
JUICE FASTING, DETOXIFYING, AND CLEANSING

Juice cleanses are known to be a good way to kick-start and reboot your health, . . .

Juice fasting, detoxifying, and cleansing is popular around the world. Not only is this a way to take your health into your own hands, but you can empower yourself and improve your health with just a little effort. When a doctor hands you a prescription, you simply fill it and follow whatever directions he or she says. You can look at a cleansing in much the same way—but this is a prescription you fill at the supermarket or farmer's market, and you simply follow good juicing practices. This prescription can always be refilled when needed. But, the truth is, routine cleansings may keep you from needing to take prescription drugs, and may even ward off a hospital stay. Success comes in steps, and cleansing is the first step of a long and healthy life.

The Good News about Juice Cleanses

Fasting has been around for thousands of years. Historically, fasting was done for spiritual renewal. More recently, fasting is done for therapeutic reasons. In the early years of therapeutic fasting, a water-only treatment was the norm. Indeed, water fasting done for a short period of time is good therapy, provided you work with a professional and get physical and emotional rest during the process. Water fasting is not recommended if you have been taking toxic drugs or certain chemotherapeutic agents, as a water-only fast can cause damage to the kidneys in these circumstances.

Juice fasting, unlike water-only fasting, allows you to continue with your daily routine. That being said, each person's body is different and each of us has to find our own way when it comes to juice fasting, detoxifying, and cleansing. This is why you should be flexible when following a juice cleansing program. Flexibility in which juice program you choose, which juices you choose, and how long you want to cleanse is key. It all works as long as you "fill the prescription" and "follow directions."

Once on a juice fast program, a step-by-step process will help you start to regain energy and vitality, which will encourage you to complete the cleansing program. Each step you take toward bettering your health will certainly make a difference as you continue your journey to learn how to trust and heal your body. The body and mind you have are yours to take care of and nurture. If you do a good job, your body will respond and can keep you going into a healthy and active old age. If we neglect them, we can expect the opposite.

Adding a juice to your daily diet is a gateway to better health. It is the best way to consume your daily-required amount of nutrients, which helps you stay healthy. Juice cleanses are known to be a good way to kick-start and reboot your health, because cleanses remove toxins, pollutants, and preservatives from the body.

Juice cleanses work well for just about everyone. Many people claim to have increased energy and vitality after a juice cleanse. Some people lose weight, and others learn how their body feels when it's working at optimum performance. There are many cases of men and women receiving approval from their doctors to cut back or even discontinue medication during or after a cleansing. Sleep typically improves, more liveliness is usually gained, and boundless energy can be experienced. People who have completed a juice cleanse have reported better dispositions and less depression.

The Theory behind Cleansing

Although juice cleansing and daily juicing are both good ways to improve your health, they should be just a part of a balanced diet that is based primarily on whole organic plant-based fruits and vegetables. Being healthy is a lifestyle choice and juice cleansing is just part of a commitment to eating a healthy diet, exercising, having a positive mental attitude, sleeping well, relaxing with intent, and enjoying life.

A good quality cleanse replaces your daily food intake with juices that are made from organic produce. Juice cleanses can last anywhere from three days to a week. Some people like to juice cleanse longer, especially if they have specific goals that include weight loss or the desire to reduce inflammation or cutting back on medications. The theory behind cleanses is this: When our bodies are not burdened with the task of digesting food, toxins are released. Juicing helps the body to flush away toxins quickly out of the body, and even a cleanse that lasts just a few days can help detoxify.

A juice cleanse won't help your body magically remove all the waste you've built up over the years, but it is a good start. This is to say, taking part in a juice cleanse, and then going back to unhealthy eating patterns makes no sense. But starting to clean up your diet after a juice cleanse, while making long-lasting lifestyle changes, does make sense. Over time you will come to feel that a clean diet is the most natural choice. When we frequently consume a plant-based diet, in effect we are cleansing it with every meal, and this helps our bodies function at a high level.

We take in and absorb chemicals daily. Some of these chemicals can come from our food, especially if that food is processed or inorganic. We consume other toxins when we imbibe alcohol to excess or inhale smoke. Other chemicals come to us from the air we breathe and the water we drink. We absorb toxins from the products we use on our bodies, and we also get them from cleaning supplies we use in our homes. Toxins that build up in our body can weaken our immune system, cause inflammation, and invite other chronic illnesses to take hold.

We expect our kidneys, liver, and colon to do the job they were designed to do, which is filter out toxins and waste. But modern life, with its easy temptations toward unhealthy habits and little indiscretions, are too much for these organs to completely handle. Giving them a little help once in a while with a juice cleanse is a good thing.

If you are taking prescription drugs, speak with your doctor or holistic practitioner before attempting any juice cleanse. For most people, a short three-day cleanse should not be dangerous in any way; nonetheless, it's best to consult your physician before starting. Pregnant or breast-feeding mothers should not do a juice cleanse.

Which Is Better When Fasting: Juicing or Blending?

A juice cleanse is a time to give your digestive system a complete rest. For this reason, juicing for a cleansing is better than blending. Juice bars and professional juice cleansing companies use a juice extractor to make juices for cleanses. In other words, blended green smoothies are not on the juice cleanse menu.

Blenders leave the plant fibers in the juice. Therefore, with blended drinks your body is digesting food and is not being relieved of this task. Moreover, particles in blended drinks that need to be digested may stimulate your appetite, and that in turn may make you hungry during the cleansing period.

If you only own a blender, strain the juice through a nut milk bag. You can purchase such a bag at your health food store or online. Alternatively, you can purchase a paint strainer bag at your hardware store. Both strainer bags and nut milk filter bags can be found on my website shop at YoungOnRawFood.com.

To Cleanse or Not to Cleanse, That Is the Question

Before starting a juice cleanse, you need to determine why you want to do a cleansing. Your goal could be to lose weight or to rid your body of an accumulation of little indiscretions gained from food, drink, or medications. Your goal could be to heal an illness or disease, or just to have more energy and vitality. Whatever your mission is, make it a strong one, a commitment you will not break.

If you can't make a good case for doing a cleansing, then old addictive eating habits will win out and you might just not complete the cleanse. The mind can play tricks on your body, giving hunger signals when your body is not hungry at all. We are creatures of habit, and you probably have certain times and locations that you associate with a meal. These times and places might include a sandwich shop you pass on the way to work, or your comfortable seat in front of the television when you come home. These are events and places where you usually have a snack or meal, and they make you feel hungry, even if you really aren't. These associations will tempt you to eat during a cleansing. In order not to succumb to these temptations, you must remember that you are not just cleansing your body, but your habits and your mind as well. Moments of temptation are opportunities to remind yourself of your commitment and why

you have made the decision to rid yourself of toxins and improve your health.

Distractions are good while cleansing. A walk or bicycle ride, a chat with friends, or a hobby will take your mind off eating. Even reading a book is a great distraction from this mental hunger, as long as it's not a cookbook. It takes three days to get the hang of cleansing, just when it's time to stop. This is why longer cleansings are easier in many ways.

FLEXIBILITY

Cleansing does not have to be an all-or-nothing endeavor. Certainly, you can drink only juice for a complete detoxifying cleanse. But you can also choose to do a modified starter cleanse by adding smoothies, salads, and soups (but no oils or fats) to your daily diet. You can choose when to start and end your cleanse. You can also choose not to do a cleanse. Whatever your choice, if you choose to cleanse, start the process by including green drinks into your daily diet. Once you are used to this healthy habit of daily juicing, a cleanse might be easier to complete.

Quick Description of Three Cleanses

Here are given three proven detoxifying cleansing programs. (For complete descriptions, see Full Cleanse Plan Descriptions on page 270.)

CLEANSE #1: EASY 3-DAY DETOXIFYING CLEANSE PLAN.

This plan is recommend if you are new to juicing and cleansing. You will be choosing from a list of easy juice recipes, and you will consume six to seven 16-ounce juices daily. Recipe servings will vary from 12–16 ounces. The Easy 3-Day Detoxifying Cleanse is also good for those who have an extra-busy schedule and less time to make more involved juices that the General 3-Day Detoxifying Cleanse program requires. Compared to other

cleanse plans, the Easy cleanse takes less time to make juices, and may be less expensive because less produce is used. You can either follow the directions of this plan exactly or you can add any juice from any of the other two cleanse programs.

Many of the suggestions in the Easy 3-Day Detoxifying Cleanse can be mixed and matched with the General or the Short Shot cleanse programs.

CLEANSE #2: SHORT SHOT 3- TO 5-DAY DETOXIFYING CLEANSE PLAN.

This plan calls for an 8-ounce juice every two hours from any of the juice cleanse recipes. Juices, flavored waters (see page 290), decaffeinated herbal teas, and Vegetable Broth (see page 274) are suggested. The 8-ounce method allows you to be satisfied and get enough nutrients, but at the same time the juices are quicker to prepare because of the smaller 8-ounce size. This cleanse also allows flexibility: If you feel hungry enough to have a full 16-ounce juice at any time of the day, you can do so.

CLEANSE #3: GENERAL 3– TO 5-DAY DETOXIFYING CLEANSE PLAN.

This plan includes directions for an additional 6–10 days of cleansing, if desired. This cleanse allows you to have six to seven 16-ounce juices daily. This program calls for flavored waters (see page 290), decaffeinated herb teas, and Vegetable Broth (see page 274). This cleanse is good for beginners and experienced juicers alike. This cleanse also allows you the flexibility to mix and match the juices you like, or you can simply follow along in the order that recipes are written.

Helping You Choose Which Cleanse

Your goals and the needs of your body will determine the sort of cleanse you should try. Are you trying to lose weight, gain energy, or rid yourself medication? If so, choose a program that suits your needs. It may be helpful to stick with one program for the three days. Then again, you may decide to mix and match programs. Regardless, establish a routine that works with your lifestyle and schedule.

Take your schedule into consideration when deciding to start a cleanse. Can you arrange to have three days where you do not have to dine out with others? Is there a special occasion you need to attend? Will you be making food for other family members? Make sure you are starting at the right time for your lifestyle. If you need to lunch with others, you might consider bringing your juice along with an herbal tea bag for an extra drink. This way you can be social and still enjoy your cleanse. Being social is important, so don't let it stop you from proceeding with a cleansing program. Remember, juicing and cleansing is a lifestyle so find ways to fit them naturally into your lifestyle.

The following four points will help you in deciding which cleanse is most appealing to you:

1. Starting with a one-day juice cleanse is a good way to determine if juicing for more days might work for you. Sometimes the first day is easy but not always. Depending on your health, the first day could be challenging. If that first day seems easy enough, then you might want to continue into the second day, and so forth. A full-day juice cleanse consists of six to seven juices daily depending on your weight, height, and caloric needs. Use your own judgment in deciding what amount to drink daily. If you are full at six juices daily, then that is the proper amount. If one day you need an extra juice, it's perfectly fine to do so.

2. Compared to a one-day cleanse, a three-day cleanse releases more toxins, brings you more energy, and better improves your mental clarity. A three-day cleanse will help your skin and

digestion improve. The third day of a cleanse is typically when you might start feeling great. This happens because any discomforts from the first couple of days start to subside on that third day. Three days will give you a good chance to go forward for five to seven days of cleansing to detoxify more deeply.

3. If you don't think juicing alone will work for you, you could try incorporating salads and soups along with juices into your diet. This is a good plan if you prepare food for others in your home or if you are used to consuming meat, potatoes, and processed foods. This type of modified maintenance plan might be easier on your mind too. Detoxification will take place during this program provided that you do not use oils, fats, meat, dairy products, white flour, sugar, or gluten products. A plant-based eating plan is recommended, and your daily diet might consist of a morning juice; a juice snack; a salad for lunch with herbs and orange, lemon, or apple juice dressing; another midday juice snack; and a warm juice soup for dinner. Lemon and water and decaffeinated herbal teas are suggested, accompanied with 64 ounces of water to stay hydrated.

4. Another alternative to a complete detoxifying cleanse is to start adding a green juice every morning on an empty stomach. Sip it slowly, even if it means you have to take some with you wherever you need to go. At lunchtime have a large salad with a variety of vegetables. For the dressing, use herbs and lemon juice, orange juice, or apple juice. Have what you consider to be a healthy dinner. Snack on veggies or fruit when you are hungry and stay away from all processed foods. This method could prepare you to move forward with a complete detoxifying cleanse. The idea is to keep moving forward in improving your health habits even if you must take one step at a time. One conscious healthy thing you do for yourself every day can add up to a lifetime of better health.

How to Start a Juice Cleanse

Are you ready to clean house? If you've decided to give a juice cleanse a try, here are some tips to help get you started.

Cleansing is not for growing children, pregnant women, or nursing mothers. Keep in mind that when animals in the wild are ill they go off and fast. Domesticated animals, when ill, are taken to a veterinarian and given massive doses of medication, and the same goes for humans. Most people can go on a short juice cleanse and experience good results.

Before you start your cleanse, prepare ahead for about three days. Avoid processed or packaged foods, sugar, meat, dairy, coffee, alcohol, and smoking. Eat lighter foods like salads, soups, and steamed vegetables. Complete any projects that need completion so you can focus on your cleanse.

To be prepared, make sure you have time to make the juices you will need on a daily basis. Also be sure you have time to rest during cleansing. Don't choose to cleanse during a time when you are under stress, dealing with emotional problems, or are experiencing a major crisis. If possible, find a juicing buddy, a friend or family member, to do the cleansing with you.

HOW TO SHOP FOR A JUICE CLEANSE

It's advisable that you have all the produce you need in-house before starting your cleanse. If you don't have your produce ready to go, it is easy to get tempted to discontinue the cleanse early. Choose your juice recipes and make a shopping list. If possible, purchase local organic produce at a farmer's market. You can also shop at health food stores or conventional stores that carry organic produce, if that is more convenient.

The idea of cleansing is to detoxify chemicals and pesticides from your body, so choose organic whenever possible. Ideally, a juice cleanse should be made with organic produce. Most juices on the grocery shelves that are packaged in a carton, can, or bottle have been pasteurized and heat-treated. Frozen juice is not fresh juice. On the shelves at your local health food store you might be able to find a couple of juices that the manufacture claims are cold-processed, such that all the enzymes are intact.

In many cities today, you can find juice bars that will make your juice to order. If you can afford to purchase fresh juices, there are companies that deliver juice right to your door for a 3- to 10-day cleanse. If you own a juicer or blender and have the time, make your own organic juice.

HOW TO STORE PRODUCE

Planning ahead is the secret to making a juice cleanse go smoothly. If you are doing a short three-day cleanse, the most efficient way is to start with a clean refrigerator. You will be surprised how much room you will need. When you arrive home from shopping, wash all your produce and wrap each day's produce in paper towels and place them into gallon zipper-seal plastic storage bags. Mark the bag with a permanent marker pen noting which day the produce is to be used.

Do not follow this plan for longer than a three-day cleanse as the vegetables and greens will decay more quickly when washed. For longer cleanses, wrap unwashed produce in paper towels and store in plastic zipper-seal storage bags or containers. Unwashed produce lasts longer as there is little moisture to rot the food. Make a note of the day and date on each bag with a permanent marker. Most food should last five to six days if the above storage directions are followed. Take freshness into consideration when shopping for produce.

HOW TO PREPARE VEGETABLES AND FRUITS FOR A JUICE CLEANSING

Thoroughly wash fruits and vegetable in purified water. Scrub each vegetable and rinse off. Peel any inorganic produce. Cut root ends off carrots. Cut brown ends off celery. Do not use any limp or old greens because they will not provide the proper amount of vitamins or liquid.

It's worth noting that there is controversy concerning whether or not to juice apple seeds. Apple seeds contain amygdalin, a cyanide compound that degrades into hydrogen cyanide when metabolized. For most people, it would take an enormous number of apple seeds to cause any problems. Your body can detoxify seeds in small numbers. If this news concerns you, core apples before juicing.

WHEN TO MAKE JUICES

It's always best to drink juices directly after juicing. But if you don't have time to make all your juices in the mornings, don't worry, you can juice in the evening and store it in a tightly closed container and refrigerate. (See page 35 for proper juice storing.) Make enough juice for one full day at a time. If you own a hydraulic cold press juicer, the juice you make will keep for 72 hours if stored and refrigerated properly.

How to Complete a Juice Cleanse

Make a solid commitment to better your health. Look at cleansing as a way to heal and take time for you.

Write down any emotions that might arise during cleansing.

Ease up on your workouts, but take a short walk daily and stretch or do some light yoga.

Headaches are normal for some people during a juice cleanse, and so are cravings. Drink a little water or a few sips of juice if this happens. Lemon and water and decaffeinated herbal teas are acceptable during a juice cleanse. Be sure to drink some water after you consume each juice so that you stay hydrated. In addition, drink an 8-ounce glass of water between each juice. This is not an option! Staying hydrated is vital for flushing out toxins.

If you rise later in the morning and go to bed late, there is no need to change your routine in order to stay with your juice cleanse. Simply consume your juice according to a schedule that works for you.

Try to drink at least five juices daily. Do not let yourself get hungry. For the majority of people, drinking a juice every two hours will help them feel full and keep their metabolism steady. Each juice plan suggested in this book should deliver you enough daily calories. But if you need more calories, or less, than what is suggested here, that's fine. Everyone on a juice cleanse needs to make personal adjustments to determine how much juice works for them. If you are new to juice cleaning, do what you can to follow one of the plans detailed in this book, mindful that you can adjust your consumption levels at any time. Just don't go hungry. Don't try to drink less juice thinking that consuming less calories makes for a better juice cleanse. A sudden and drastic reduction in calories is not good for your metabolism. And because you are not giving your body enough nutrients if you skimp on calories, you may want to stop the juice cleanse too early.

While on a juice cleanse, it might be best to stay away from any associations with solid food. Preparing food for others could encourage you to eat. Even working in the vegetable garden could stimulate the desire to eat. If you find yourself thinking about solid food, go for a walk or distract yourself. Chances are the feeling will pass. A cup of warm tea can do the trick. You could also try having the General #9 juice from the General Cleanse (see page 280) slightly warmed. I have found that this particular juice eases the desire for food. Putting the #9 in a bowl just like you would soup and eating it with a spoon might give you a satisfied feeling.

During these cleansing times, chances are it's not your body that is hungry. Rather, your mind and old habits are stimulating your desire for solid food. A strong commitment can keep you going during these times, so make sure you have a strong commitment when starting a cleanse.

Not everyone feels hungry during a juice cleansing, and many people feel more energized immediately. Even so, other people experience physical symptoms that concern them, including headaches and fatigue. Some people also experience personal fears, or feel judged by friends or family members. Feelings or doubts may come over you while your body detoxifies. When in doubt, remember your commitments for bettering your health.

14 STARTING SUGGESTIONS THAT ARE GOOD FOR ALL CLEANSE PLANS

The following suggestions will help with the detoxifying process. Do as many as possible during your cleanse.

1. Upon arising, use a tongue scraper (or invert a spoon) and scrape any toxic buildup from the back of your tongue. Brush your teeth and tongue with baking soda mixed with half the amount of salt. Floss as usual.

2. Dry-brush your body before bathing. Purchase a natural vegetable-fiber brush at a health food store. Always work from the extremities towards the heart. Work from the feet up, then from the fingertips toward the heart. Brush everything but your face. Do not use much pressure the first few times. A soft rotary motion is sufficient. Easy does it so your body gets used to this kind of treatment. This should take no more than 7–10 minutes. Take a hot shower, ending with a quick cold rinse. This process helps to release toxins from the skin

and helps with circulation. Brushing stimulates nerve endings and glands, and keeps your skin looking young and vibrant. For face brushing, purchase a small brush, or an electric one if you prefer, that is made especially for faces.

3. It is important to detoxify your mind of negative thoughts from the past and present, and then put them into a psychic wastebasket. When ready, toss it away. Mindful acts of releasing your negative thoughts will be a good exercise while you detoxify your body.

4. After your shower, drink an 8-ounce glass of water with the juice from one lemon. If you feel hungry, or are used to having coffee or tea each morning, wait 15–20 minutes after your lemon drink, and then warm 8 ounces of the Vegetable Broth (see page 274) or have a warm tea.

5. In ½–1 hour after your lemon water, have your first juice. If this is your first juice cleanse, you might dilute your chosen cleansing breakfast juice with good purified water. Diluting is suggested for beginners so that they can help their bodies get used to juicing.

6. At midmorning, have a cup of herbal decaffeinated tea. Do not boil the water to a full boil; rather, heat it up just enough to produce tiny bubbles. Drink organic decaffeinated teas only; green, chamomile, and peppermint teas are good choices.

7. Two hours after your first juice, have your second juice, which can also be diluted if desired. If you have time, this would be a good time to walk or do other light stretching exercises.

8. If you have access to a steam bath, sauna, or massage, it would be advisable during your cleanse to do at least one or more of these activities if possible. Do not steam or sauna very long, just enough to release sweat and toxins. Massages stimulate the lymphatic system, which helps clear the body of waste buildup and promotes detoxification and elimination. Massage is also a good way to rest and restore the body.

9. Between lunch and dinner juices, have another cup of herbal tea, Vegetable Broth (page 274), or a small juice.

10. In the early evening (dinner), have another glass of juice.

11. Mid-evening, if you are hungry, have a juice, tea, or Vegetable Broth.

12. If you stay up late and feel any hunger, you might consider a small cup of warm Vegetable Broth before bedtime.

13. Drink at least eight glasses of water throughout the day to stay hydrated and help flush away toxins.

14. Be sure to honor, nurture, and appreciate yourself for taking this journey to improve your health and mental attitude. Smile at that person in the mirror and tell yourself you are beautiful or handsome just the way you are. This might seem uncomfortable at first, but keep working on it. This is a very important step in finding self-love, acceptance, appreciation, and gratitude for who you are.

Release More Toxins

If you can get a colonic from a professional, do so. If you are up to it, you can give yourself an enema to release more toxins and any old buildup in your system.

How to End a Juice Cleanse— Important!

After a juice cleanse your body will need a bit of time to adjust and shift back to eating and digesting. Sometimes cravings for all your favorite foods arise. But if you eat a full meal right after completing your juice cleanse, you will probably experience a lot of discomfort. You will be better off if you move slowly and avoid heavy foods at first because your digestive system will have slowed down during the cleansing.

Increase and build up your food intake a little at a time for a few days. Mono foods are best to eat when coming off cleansing. Mono foods are one single type of food that is eaten as a meal. For example, only watermelon, only apples, and so forth. The best foods to eat at the end of a juice cleanse are foods that have a high water content. These foods include apples, oranges, tomatoes, cucumbers, watermelon, grapefruit, pears, grapes, and mangoes. Continue juicing if you like, but go slowly when introducing solid food into your system again. Do not eat a solid, cooked meal for at least a day after completing a cleansing.

Eat slowly and chew everything very well. Don't eat heavy foods like pastas, potatoes, rice, or beans. Avoid dairy for a few days, as well as meat. Don't eat junk food or any processed foods. Once your body gets back to digesting, it's okay to incorporate other foods. However, it is recommended that you cut out processed or junk food altogether. The days after cleansing are a good time to take a look at a new healthy way of eating. If you want to improve your diet and start including more plant-based foods, this would be a good time to move in that direction.

It's Time to Start Juice Cleansing

The following juice cleanses are measured for a juicer, not a blender. If you are using a blender and all the ingredients do not fit into your blender, adjust as necessary. Filtered water must be added to blended juices. Strain blended juices for juice cleansing. As mentioned earlier, you are cleansing to release toxins and relax your digestive system. Fiber keeps the digestive system working and can possibly create the feeling of hunger. If you decide not to strain the blended drinks you make, then go ahead and drink your juice with the fiber in it. It is better to cleanse with blended juices than not to cleanse at all.

Full Cleanse Plan Descriptions

Measurements for each juice are somewhere between 12 and 16 ounces. The type of juicer you use and the varying size or water content of your produce make it impossible to give exact juicing yields. If a drink is a little short, then add more ingredients or fill the container to the top with a little filtered water.

CLEANSE #1: EASY 3-DAY DETOXIFYING CLEANSE PLAN

Follow each recipe in order, or mix and match from any of the listed recipes. Consume six to seven juices or soup broth throughout the day and drink water in between. Juices will be 12–16 ounces, more or less. Since some of these juices yield a smaller amount of juice, you might feel the need to consume an extra juice or two, which is okay to do.

There may be times during the day when a 16-ounce juice might be too much for you to drink. On such occasions, a 12-ounce juice might seem to be more appropriate. Do what works best for your appetite and listen to your body. If you wait too long in between juices, you might not be able to keep your metabolism steady, and you will soon feel hungry. Be sure to drink enough juices daily, approximately every two hours.

This cleanse is for beginners or seasoned juice fans alike. What is great about this cleanse is the simplicity in preparation. A limited amount of ingredients are used in each juice, and they take less time to make as compared to other recipes. This cleanse will provide you with a variety of nutrients that will be satisfying. It will be easy to prepare and should encourage you to come back again for another cleanse. You can choose juices from the Easy 3-Day Cleanse or you can mix in some from the General 3-Day Cleanse.

SHOPPING LIST FOR THE EASY 3-DAY DETOXIFYING CLEANSE PLAN

There is no definitive way to determine to the letter exactly how much produce you will need because the size of vegetables and fruits vary. What type of produce you purchase and the amount of each will depend on if you choose a variety of juice recipes or if you duplicate some. The most accurate way to determine what your personal needs will be is to use the Juice Measurement Scale (see page 79), and then choose the juices you want to make. I recommend you use the Juice Measurement Scale to determine approximately how much juice you will get from the basic ingredients (e.g., celery, cucumber, or apple), make your grocery list, and shop for three days' worth of ingredients. If you don't want to make a list of your own, you can use the one provided.

Detox Fruit

∙ ∙ ∙ ∙ ∙ ∙ ∙ ∙ ∙ ∙ ∙ ∙ ∙ ∙ ∙ ∙ ∙ ∙ ∙ ∙ ∙

If you are unable to use all organic produce for the following recipes, then peel, scrub, or soak fruits and vegetables very well before juicing.

This following list will carry one person through two days of juicing if you make one of each juice cleanse recipe. For day 3, choose which juices you want to duplicate and then add what is needed to your 3-day shopping list. There will be enough of some produce for all 3 days, but depending on which juices you choose to duplicate you may need to add more produce for day 3.

3-DAY DETOXIFYING CLEANSE PLAN SHOPPING LIST

6 apples, Fuji

6 large apples, green

1 large or 2 medium beet

2 baskets berries

2 cups broccoli

1 teaspoon cardamom

21 carrots

1½ cups cashews

1 small head cauliflower

1 large bunch or 2 medium celery

a few pinches cinnamon

3 largecucumbers

1 medium piece ginger

1 bunch kale

3 lemons

1 lime

maple syrup or stevia to taste

1 medium bunch mint

6 oranges

3 bunches parsley

1 pineapple

1 large bunch romaine lettuce

2 bunches spinach

1 basket strawberries

2 beans or 1 tablespoon extract vanilla bean or extract

1 small watermelon

1 small bunch watercress

Recipes for Easy 3-Day Detoxifying Cleanse Plan

Feel free to add ginger, turmeric, lemon, or mint to any drink. Note to beginners: If you have any stomach discomfort, you can use a little filtered water to dilute the juice until your body's digestive system corrects itself. It's natural that our digestion has to reboot itself while we detoxify and change eating habits.

Since Easy #1, has no greens to neutralize the natural sugars in carrots and oranges, it's best to have that drink in the morning. You will be consuming a smaller juice portion, which is perfect for this sweeter combination. If you want to increase the amount of juice, add filtered water to dilute. Easy #1 is also a great pick-me-up juice. Easy #1 is not recommended for diabetics, so please substitute with any other juice from this cleansing plan.

EASY #1

2 oranges

4 carrots

EASY #2

1–2 apples

4 stalks celery

3 kale leaves, stems removed

1 cucumber

3 mint sprigs

EASY #3

2 Granny Smith (green) apples

5 carrots

4 romaine leaves or 2 handfuls of any dark leafy greens

1-inch piece of ginger

EASY #4

½ pineapple

4 carrots

2 cups spinach

1–2 mint sprigs

EASY #5

2 Granny Smith (green) apples

3 celery stalks

4 romaine leaves

½ lemon, juiced

EASY #6

1 orange

3 carrots

1 handful of strawberries

2 cups spinach or 5 romaine leaves

EASY #7

½ cucumber

1 Fuji apple

4 celery stalks

½ lemon, juiced

EASY #8

¼ of a watermelon—organic with rind;
if nonorganic, remove rind

1 lime, juiced

2–3 mint sprigs

EASY #9

1 Granny Smith (green) apple

1 cucumber

4 celery stalks

2 kale leaves, stems removed, or collard leaves

EASY #10

1 orange, juiced

1 Granny Smith (green) apple

1 lemon, juiced

3 carrots

EASY #11

Easy Juice Popsicle (for a treat). (Other sweet juices can also be made into popsicles.)

Juice from 2–3 apples

2 handfuls strawberries, 2 peaches,
or other berries

1 lemon, juiced

Feel free to toss in a little leafy greens

DIRECTIONS

Blend apple juice with strawberries and lemon. Add water as needed. Strain and freeze in Popsicle molds.

EASY #12 VEGETABLE BROTH

Vegetable broth contains high vitamins and minerals including magnesium, calcium trace minerals, sodium, and potassium.

INGREDIENTS

1 cup celery, roughly chopped

1 cup beets, peeled and roughly chopped

1 small onion

2 cups combined of any or all of the following: turnips and tops, beet tops, watercress, spinach, parsley, broccoli, or cauliflower

DIRECTIONS

Scrub all vegetables, leaving skin on carrots. In a large five- to six-quart pot, add 1½ quarts of water, and place veggies into the pot. Let water heat up, but not boil. Light simmer on lowest flame for 30 minutes while watching, so as not to boil. Turn off heat, cover pan, and let sit another one half hour or more. Strain the broth through a colander into a large bowl and discard vegetables because the flavor and nutrient value are now in the broth. Store broth in a mason jar, or similar, and refrigerate. Serve warm or room temperature. When warming, do not overheat. Salt may be added for taste.

EASY #13 PARSLEY BROTH

Juice one to two bunches of Italian parsley. Heat water almost to boiling. Put one tablespoon parsley juice in cup, pour in water, add one clove crushed garlic and a pinch of salt to taste. Stir well. Serve warm. Balance of juiced parsley can be refrigerated for one day.

EASY #14 SPOILER ALERT

The Spoiler Alert can be very satisfying during the day, even if you have just a couple of sips to ease your mind from feeling hungry. It does not have to be consumed in one setting. This little trick of a few sips can keep you on the cleansing path.

If you are allergic to nuts or prefer to leave nuts out of your cleanse, you may substitute hemp milk or one of your favorite juices for the Spoiler Alert.

Drink only one a day if needed.

INGREDIENTS

1½ cups cashew milk or hemp seed milk (see recipes page 185 & 190)

1 teaspoon vanilla extract or seeds from ½ vanilla bean

Pinch of cinnamon

⅛ teaspoon of cardamom, (optional)

A small amount of stevia, Medjool date, or maple syrup to taste

CLEANSE #2: SHORT SHOT 3-DAY DETOXIFYING CLEANSE PLAN

This plan is good for people who might prefer a short 8-ounce juice every two hours instead of a larger 12- to 16-ounce juice. One major reason for a Short Shot cleanse program is convenience. Less juice is consumed so it is quickly prepared. Drinking an 8-ounce juice every two hours helps the metabolism to remain steady and the stomach feel full.

Infused waters (see page 290), herbal teas, and Vegetable Broth (see page 274) can be consumed anytime in between, along with filtered water after each juice. This plan allows for complete freedom to choose which juices you will consume from any of the detoxifying cleanse programs. Just cut the recipes in half. If you feel hungry, feel free to have a larger juice at any time during the day. It's important to stay hydrated and drink water in between juices.

If you decide to try a longer detoxifying period, choose a variety of juices from any of the programs.

CLEANSE #3: GENERAL 3-DAY DETOXIFYING CLEANSE PLAN

Before starting, please read the section How to Start a Juice Cleanse on page 265.

This plan contains a list of nutrient-dense juice recipes. Feel free to choose any juice on this list throughout the day. This plan suggests six to seven juices daily. Additionally, herbal decaffeinated teas may be consumed along with infused waters and Vegetable Broth (see page 274 for recipe).

Choose any drink that sounds good to you and duplicate it a second time if you like. Juicing can be very personal and your taste buds will identify your favorites. To ensure that you get all the nutrients you need daily, you must consume a variety of juices. Feel free to add more or less of any vegetable, green, or fruit to a recipe. Be creative. Mix and match any drinks you enjoy for days one through three, and longer if desired.

You can cleanse for more than three days, which would allow the body to go further in the detoxification process; however most busy people can only easily handle one to three days. If you have the time and courage to do more than a three-day juice cleanse, then give it a try. I know people who have done extensive cleanses for 60 days or longer with great results. If you choose to do a long cleanse, consult your doctor so that he or she can check your vitals throughout this process.

If you can only do one day, that's all right. One day is better than none at all. If you can commit to three days, you will have great results with detoxification. Three days can improve your energy level, eliminate stored wastes, boost mental clarity, and improve circulation.

Start each day with a glass of water with juice from half a lemon. This alkaline drink will help balance your digestive system. If you are new to juicing and eat a standard Western diet, it might be best for you to start with a three-day cleanse. This cleanse will encourage you to want more. See How to Start a Juice Cleanse (page 265).

Warning:
You may become addicted
to juicing!

Fill the juice container with filtered water after drinking each juice and drink all the water before the next scheduled juice. It is important that you drink at least 64 ounces of water daily during a juice cleanse in order to flush out as much toxins as possible. If you do not drink enough water, your cleanse will go more slowly and toxins will take longer to release.

If you can't find one of the ingredients or have an allergy to any of the ingredients, by all means replace that ingredient with another. If you don't care for a certain recipe, feel free to substitute. If kale seems bitter, try spinach, broccoli, romaine, or less kale. By adding lemon, ginger, or mint, juices become more delicious and easier to drink.

In some areas of the country it is harder to find some produce during winter months. Do your best and replace whatever you can't find. If greens are not available, try sprouting your own. Sprouting can be done year-round on your kitchen counter. Juicing sprouts is very beneficial. Sprouts are loaded with chlorophyll and protein.

On a three-day cleanse, it's best not to include any solid foods. Eating solid foods will not give your digestive system a rest. Eating solid foods will also stimulate hunger, as your body will be working to digest the solid food. A three-day cleanse is a jump-start to heal, detoxify, and help retrain your taste buds.

If during a juice cleanse you have a headache or feel tired, you should know that this is a normal part of the process. Not everyone experiences the symptoms, but if you do, simply drink more water and rest. Hang tough, your discomfort will soon pass and you will feel better.

The three-day juice cleanse detailed here is set up to give you six drinks daily. If you are of a larger stature, you might need eight juices. You can duplicate any juice you like for the extra juices.

Feel free to repeat recipes for day two except for Spoiler Alert (page 274), because this very satisfying drink contains nuts. Having a Spoiler Alert every other day is fine, but if you are looking for more weight loss you might not want to drink it as often during your cleanse. Look over all the recipes and determine which ones are most appealing to you. You should enjoy the tastes of the juices.

SHOPPING LIST FOR 3- TO 5-DAY GENERAL DETOXIFYING CLEANSE PLAN

There is no definite way to determine to the letter exactly how much produce you will require because the size of vegetables and fruits vary. You may also decide to choose a variety of juices or duplicate some. The closest way to determine what your personal needs will be is to use the Juice Measurement Scale (see page 79), and then choose the juices you want to make. I recommend that you use the Juice Measurement Scale to determine approximately how much juice you will get from the basic ingredients (e.g., celery, cucumber, or apple), make your grocery list, and then shop for three days' worth of ingredients. If you don't want to make a list of your own, you can follow the one provided here.

3- TO 5-DAY GENERAL DETOXIFYING CLEANSE PLAN SHOPPING LIST

---

12 Granny Smith apples

1 small bunch basil

2 medium beets

1 red bell pepper

1 basket berries

1 cup broccoli

10 large carrots

1½ cups cashews

2 bunches celery

1 small bunch chard

A couple of pinches cinnamon

2 cups coconut water

5 medium cucumbers

1 bulb fennel

1 bulb garlic

1 five-inch piece ginger

2 cups grapes

1 bunch kale

5 lemons

Maple syrup or stevia to taste

1 bunch mint

2 oranges

1 bunch parsley

1 Bosc pear

1 pineapple

1 bunch Romaine lettuce

1 large bunch (approximately 8 handfuls) spinach

1 medium sweet potato

2 or 3 tomatoes

1 small bunch watercress

2 vanilla beans or 1 teaspoon extract

Recipes for General 3-Day Detoxifying Cleanse Plan

All recipes make one serving.

The following cleanse recipes are very alkalizing, as a good concentration of greens are used in the juices. Feel free to mix together recipes or subtract any ingredients you don't care for. If you can't find an ingredient at your farmer's market or supermarket, replace with a similar ingredient. Experimentation is encouraged, but remember that greens are the most alkalizing ingredients.

More or Less

· · · · · · · · · · · · · · · · · · · ·

If the ingredients of one recipe make more than 16 ounces of juice, juice more ingredients to make another 16 ounces and fill another jar. If a juice is less than 16 ounces, just choose one of the ingredients in the recipe and juice until you have 16 ounces. As mentioned, all veggies and fruits are different sizes so recipe amounts might vary.

Directions for all cleansing juices: Unless different directions are given for an individual juice, juice all the ingredients in the order given. For recipes with a citrus ingredient, either peel citrus and put segments through juicer or juice separately and stir into finished drink.

GENERAL #1

3 handfuls spinach

2 celery stalks

½ medium cucumber

1 cup pineapple chunks

1 Granny Smith (green) apple

2 carrots

½ lemon, juiced

GENERAL #2

1 lemon, juiced

1 apple

Pinch of cayenne pepper

2 mint sprigs

Add filtered water if needed

GENERAL #3

1 cucumber

2 celery stalks

2 kale leaves (stems removed),
romaine lettuce, or a handful of spinach

¼ red bell pepper

1 Granny Smith (green) apple or pear

½ lemon, juiced

1-inch piece of ginger

GENERAL #4

½ cucumber

3 carrots

2 celery stalks

1 apple

½ beet

¼ piece fennel bulb

1-inch piece of ginger

GENERAL #5

2 handfuls spinach

4 romaine leaves

2 celery stalks

½ medium cucumber

1 Granny Smith (green) apple

1 orange, juiced

½ lemon, juiced

GENERAL #6

¼ medium fennel

3 celery stalks

½ cucumber

1 large Granny Smith (green) apple

1-inch piece ginger

DAY 2—GENERAL CLEANSE PLAN

GENERAL #7

½ cucumber

1 apple

2 kale leaves (stems removed), romaine lettuce, or spinach

1 cup grapes

½ cup berries

Consistency

When using berries or grapes, juice the first three ingredients and put the juice in a blender. Add grapes and berries and blend well. Depending on the water content of ingredients in this juice, a small amount of purified water may be added to the blender to make the drink the perfect consistency.

GENERAL #8

3–4 large carrots

½ beet

1 or 2 Granny Smith (green) apples

½ lemon, juiced

1-inch piece ginger or more if desired

2 handfuls spinach

GENERAL #9

2 tomatoes, seeded

1 garlic clove

½ red bell pepper

2 celery stalks

Squeeze of lemon

⅓ cup broccoli

3 stems watercress

2–3 basil leaves

Pinch of pink Himalayan salt

Pinch of oregano

Pinch of dried Italian herbs

Chili flakes (optional)

1 cup or more filtered water

GENERAL #10

4 large romaine leaves

½ cup sweet potato

¼ medium beet

1 carrot

½ cucumber

1 Granny Smith (green) apple

Smoothie Bowl

This drink is best made in a blender to keep it slightly thick. Drink as is or warm lightly for a soup. I enjoy having this in a bowl.

GENERAL #11

2 handfuls spinach

4 romaine leaves

2 chard leaves

2 celery stalks

½ cucumber

1 Granny Smith (green) apple

1 Bosc pear

½ lemon, juiced

GENERAL #12

You can get delicious healthy coconut water from the inside of a young Thai coconut (see page 186). Most health food stores will open the coconut for you. You can also purchase minimally processed or cold-processed coconut water online, such as Zico, Harmless Harvest, Taste Nirvana, or Vita Coco brands.

16 ounces coconut water

(Straight up or add mint leaves and a squeeze of lime.)

GENERAL #14

Spoiler Alert (for 2 days only out of 6 days)
(See page 274 for recipe.)

DAY 3—GENERAL CLEANSE PLAN

Choose your favorite recipes from days 1 and 2.

7- to 10-Day Detoxifying Cleanse Plan

Warning: You may need a new pair of skinny jeans!

You're a good candidate for this plan if you've previously experienced a juice cleanse. This plan is also a good choice if you already eat a healthy diet that includes salads, vegetables, and fresh fruits. If you feel the need for a deep cleansing from your fast-paced life, you should find a way to adjust your schedule for 7–10 days so that you can take the time to rest. The same is true if you want to lose weight or get off medication. Consult your health care provider before starting any plan.

For your first three days, follow the three-day juice plan. Choose your favorite juices for the balance of the 7- to 10-day plan. If you are cleansing for more than three to five days, do not purchase all juicing ingredients at once. For the extended cleanse, use the 3-day shopping list and purchase the items for each three days of the cleanse. The exception would be if you have enough room in your refrigerator to store more vegetables and fruits, then feel free shop for a longer period of time.

Before starting this plan, see How to Store Fruits and Vegetables on page 50. Berries should be placed in a container single file with a paper towel on the bottom of container to absorb moisture. Store them in the refrigerator.

Infused Waters, page 290

10

BEYOND JUICING

Making kombucha may sound a little mystifying but once you get started you will understand that it only takes a few steps to make this amazingly healthy brew.

Kombucha, infused waters, and using pulp from juicing are all part of a good health plan. Kombucha aids in digestion and infused waters helps us to consume more water with some added herbed benefits. If you've wondered what to do with the fibrous pulp from juicing, then this chapter can give you some ideas on how to turn juice pulp into healthy treats.

Kombucha

Kombucha is a fermented fizzy tea that has been around for many hundreds of years. The Chinese call it the "Immortal Health Elixir." Kombucha is made with a mixture of filtered water, organic sugar, black, green, or white tea, and the culture called a scoby. The final taste of this drink varies depending on the time allowed for fermentation and the flavoring used. Kombucha has a mild vinegar taste. It will acquire a stronger taste if left to ferment longer. Flavoring the tea after fermentation with fruit or herbs gives the brew additional flavor.

All cultured and fermented foods contain a small amount of naturally occurring alcohol. The alcohol in kombucha is normally around 0.5–3 percent. The alcohol content can be higher when it is mixed with fruit juice for flavoring and is then allowed to sit for longer periods of time in a second fermentation.

In 2010, commercial kombucha brands were pulled off the market shelves by the federal alcohol trade bureau. They tested and found the kombucha to contain more than the allowed 0.5 percent alcohol that is permitted without proper alcohol labeling. When any product is labeled alcohol, the manufacturer has to pay an alcohol tax. This higher alcohol content occurred because the product was still fermenting in the bottle, thus increasing the alcohol content.

The federal alcohol trade bureau developed guidelines for kombucha manufacturers so that fermentation would not continue in the bottle. These guidelines could mean that some commercial manufactures will utilize pasteurization, which might limit some of the benefits of kombucha. Some manufacturers paid the alcohol tax on special black label bottles, which means that you must be the proper drinking age to purchase these products. All other kombucha drinks, not marked black label, will have less alcohol content and might possibly be pasteurized. These facts provide good reasons for you to learn to make your own kombucha.

WHY DRINK KOMBUCHA?

Many health claims have been made for this elixir. These claims include curing some cancers, treating arthritis, maintaining a healthy digestive tract, preventing and healing degenerative diseases that include candida, fibromyalgia, depression, and bowel and stomach disorders.

Even if these claims stretch the truth, kombucha is nonetheless a natural detoxifier for the body and is rich in enzymes. Kombucha is a probiotic beverage, which can indeed aid and improve digestion, remove harmful chemicals from the liver, and promote enzymes and good acids in the body.

Making kombucha may sound a little mystifying when you read the directions; however, it is really quite simple. Once you get started you will understand that it only takes a few steps to make this amazingly healthy brew. Because the culture starter is alive, please follow the detailed instructions and get educated about them.

WHAT IS A SCOBY?

Scoby (aka mother or mushroom) is an acronym for "symbiotic colony of bacteria and yeast."

A scoby is a starter culture made up of an accumulation of bacteria and yeast. A starter is necessary for making kombucha. A scoby can form different pancake-like shapes. Some are smooth and rubbery, some may have holes, and others are lumpy and misshapen. They can be light brown, white, grayish, or beige in color. They are all good to use and all are "mothers" that will produce "babies" (this is where the term "mother" comes from). A scoby or mother is necessary to start fermentation. When placed in the brewing tea, a scoby can float to the top, sink, or hover in the liquid. It might produce strings of yeast that hang down into the liquid. Strings can also form on the scoby itself. These attributes all describe a healthy scoby, as strange as it may seem.

Rarely will a scoby get moldy and have to be discarded. You will know when this happens as the mold will be white or colorful and fuzzy. If the scoby dies, it will be black. Brown spots may appear on a scoby, but this is not mold. If a scoby gets moldy, toss out the whole batch of brew, including the scoby.

Kombucha cultures can be reused many times over. A new scoby will form in every batch of kombucha tea. When a batch of tea is finished and bottled, you can allow the babies to remain on the original scoby for the next brewing batch, or you can peel off the babies and pass them on to someone who may benefit from the healthy properties of kombucha. Babies can also be composted along with older cultures. If babies are not peeled off the original scoby, the culture will thicken. This is not a problem unless the culture gets too difficult to handle. There are no benefits to a thicker scoby. You can always discard the babies. Keep in mind that a scoby will grow to the size of the container it is kept in. A scoby can be cut in half, preferably with porcelain knife. If you don't have such a knife, be sure the knife you use is very clean. The scoby will heal over and form another scoby on top of the cut piece when placed into the tea brew.

STARTING A SCOBY FROM SCRATCH

If possible, get a starter from a friend who makes kombucha. A new scoby is formed with every batch, and those of us who make our own kombucha are always looking for a home for baby scobys. If you are the first on your block to make kombucha, there are a few ways you can obtain a starter. You can order a scoby/mother starter from a reputable online source, including Cultures for Health, or you can start your own from scratch.

Most health food stores carry commercial kombucha in a bottle. Starting a scoby from a store-bought kombucha is very easy. The first step is to purchase a bottle of kombucha. Pour the kombucha into a large jar or glass bowl. Do not use a metal or plastic container. Cover the container with cheesecloth or a breathable kitchen towel, and then place a rubber band around the neck of the jar to secure the cloth. Place the jar away from light for approximately two weeks. The scoby will start to grow by forming a milky film in the liquid. The scoby will thicken as the days go by. The temperature in the room will determine how quickly the scoby grows. Warmer temperatures produce a more rapidly growing scoby. When you see the scoby form into a disk (usually in about two weeks), it is time to brew tea and start the fermentation process. All utensils should be clean and sterile so as not to contaminate the brew.

INGREDIENTS NEEDED FOR MAKING KOMBUCHA

1 scoby

8 black, green, or white tea bags, regular, or decaffeinated

1 cup kombucha liquid from a prior batch, called a starter tea

1 cup organic cane sugar

Fruit or herbs to flavor the kombucha for a second fermentation

SUPPLIES NEEDED FOR MAKING KOMBUCHA

A 1-gallon glass sun tea jar or ceramic vessel. Do not use plastic, stainless steel, or other metals.

A long-handled wooden spoon for stirring; no metal.

Some cheesecloth, paint strainer bag, or cloth that allows air to circulate. It should be large enough to fit over the opening of the glass container.

A rubber band or string that is large (or small) enough to fit around the neck of the bottle to securely set the cloth.

Several 8- to 12-ounce bottles with screw tops or air-lock caps. (Bottles of this type are also used for home brewing beer.)

A plastic strainer.

Brewing Tea for Kombucha

There are two methods for brewing the tea for kombucha. One method is to make a sun tea using water that is not boiled. Another method is to make a standard tea using boiled water. Regardless of method, a scoby is added after the tea is brewed.

THE SUN TEA METHOD

Fill a 1-gallon jar with filtered water. Remove the paper tags from eight black, green, or white tea bags. Strings may be left on. Place the tea bags into the jar. Add 1 cup of organic cane sugar, stir well, and secure the lid. Set the jar in a sunny spot for a day. It is not recommended that you add brown sugar or honey to the mixture as these ingredients may slow down or even stop the fermenting process. The organic cane sugar and caffeine will be completely eaten up during the fermenting process (fermentation lives off caffeine and sugar). Tea will be ready in a few hours if set in sunlight, longer if there is no sun.

THE BOILING METHOD

Boil one half the amount of water that will fit in the sun tea jar, and then add 1 cup of organic cane sugar. Dissolve the sugar by stirring. Place eight black, green, or white tea bags with tags removed into the boiled water. Turn off the heat and let mixture cool. Pour into fermenting jar and add the balance of purified water. The tea must be cool before adding the scoby.

FERMENTING THE TEA

When the tea is finished brewing, remove the tea bags. Slip the scoby into the jar with 1 cup of starter tea from a prior batch. The process of adding the mature acidified liquid is important because it ensures that no mold forms. Once you place the scoby into the tea, the scoby might float to the top or drop to the bottom or on its side. Do not be concerned if it sinks to the bottom as it will rise back up to the top in a couple of days. Save the balance of the starter tea. Doing so allows you to return the scoby to a safe place after the fermentation is complete.

Cover the jar with a piece of cheesecloth, paint bag, or any breathable cloth that allows air to circulate. The aim here is to keep pesky fruit flies or mold spores out of the brew. Put a rubber band or tie around the cloth at the neck of the jar to keep the cloth secure. Place the jar away from sunlight in a warm location, and put a sticker

or tape on the jar with the date that the brew started. Dating the bottle is important so you know how long the tea has been fermenting.

In approximately 10–14 days, remove the cloth and taste the tea using a wooden spoon. Metal is not advised as it might contaminate the liquid. The kombucha should not taste too sweet or too vinegary. The warmer the temperature, the faster the kombucha ferments. During warmer times, check kombucha in 5–6 days. When the sugar taste has dissipated, fermentation has taken place. Let your taste buds decide if enough sugar has been converted.

When you are happy with the fermented taste of the kombucha, it's ready to drink. You can decide at this time to bottle and refrigerate, or if a second fermentation with flavorings is desired. A second fermentation increases the carbonation and lactic acid. It also adds a small amount of the alcohol content, around 0.1–0.2 percent. For reference, beer contains about 4 percent alcohol and wine about 7 percent.

FLAVORING KOMBUCHA

A second fermentation allows flavorings to be added to the kombucha, giving it a delicious taste while producing more carbonation. Any fruit, vegetable, or herb can be used to flavor kombucha.

Flavoring kombucha adds more variety and enhances the taste. Sugars help kombucha to fizz and carbonate, so using something sweet for flavoring is suggested. Use ¼ cup fruit to each 16 ounces of kombucha tea. Both frozen and fresh fruit work well.

Using a large mason jar, add ¼ cup fruit, and then pour in 16 ounces of kombucha tea. Let the mixture marinate 24 hours. This method allows you to experiment with a variety of flavors using the fermented tea from the 1-gallon jar.

FLAVORING SUGGESTIONS

If using frozen fruit, place in a bowl and let it partially or thoroughly thaw. Use both the fruit and the liquid when marinating. If using fresh fruit, add ¼ cup to mason jars and pour in the kombucha tea.

Cherries, raspberries, blackberries, strawberries, grapes, mango, pomegranate, ginger, and lemon with a dash of honey all make delicious kombucha. Do not include the rind of citrus fruits as citrus rinds give off a bitter taste. Experimentation is suggested.

If using liquid juice instead of whole fruit, skip directly to second fermentation process.

SECOND FERMENTATION

After 24 hours have passed, the kombucha will have picked up the fruit flavors. Strain flavored kombucha tea with a plastic strainer, not metal, directly into an airtight clip bottle. Strained fruit will be soft, and if there is any flavor left in them they can be used in smoothies. However, in most cases the flavor will have been extracted. Fill bottles to about 2 inches from the top—carbonation pressurizes the bottle, and the bottle could explode if is filled all the way to the top.

Set bottles on the counter out of the way. It may take anywhere from 3–5 days for more carbonation to occur. Release the tops once a day during this time. Taste to see if the carbonation is to your liking. When desired level of carbonation is achieved, refrigerate bottles. Although carbonation is slowed down once refrigerated, you may need to release the cap every couple days. Open bottles carefully as carbonation will not stop entirely.

After adding the flavoring, label the bottles with the flavor. This allows you to learn what your favorite flavors are. If you plan to make another batch of kombucha immediately, add the date to the bottles label so you know which batch of kombucha to consume first.

HOW TO STORE A SCOBY WHEN NOT MAKING KOMBUCHA

Once you start making kombucha, you will more than likely make one batch after another. Eventually, for one reason or another, you might have to stop. To keep your culture alive, it is best to leave it submerged in a jar or glass container with enough sugared tea to keep it covered. Cover the container with cheesecloth held in place with a rubber band and leave it on the kitchen counter. The cheesecloth will allow the culture to breathe. This method is good if the time frame is less than six weeks.

Longer breaks are a little more difficult to accomplish but are not impossible. If you take a vacation from making kombucha for a period of time longer than six weeks and want to keep the scoby alive, leave the scoby in a full-size jar of brewed kombucha tea. This will keep the scoby alive. When ready to use again, discard the brewed tea as it will have a strong vinegar taste. You might like to use the vinegar brew for making a salad dressing, or you can just toss it out.

Another option for holding the scoby for more than several weeks is to keep a holding jar. This holding jar can sit on the kitchen counter. Every 4–6 weeks discard some of the tea brew and put some fresh sugared tea in its place. Up to 80 percent replacement is fine. The fresh sugar will provide the scoby with all the nutrients it needs to survive.

Another method is to place the scoby in a fresh batch of brewed tea and refrigerate the brew. The cold will slow the fermentation process and put the scoby in hibernation. When ready to use, toss the tea and put the scoby into a new batch of sugared tea and proceed as usual. Freezing is not an option.

Infused Waters

Water is a vital part of our bodies. We need to drink at least eight glasses a day, approximately 64 ounces. Drinking infused waters is a helpful way to keep hydrated; they are beautiful, tasty, and inviting. They also make a great addition to any meal or party. Infused waters can have healing properties when they are infused with herbal ingredients.

Two or three large mason jars of infused water is a sufficient amount to drink on a daily basis. Room temperature waters are best for headaches. For iced waters, store infused waters in refrigerator.

Infused waters are best when they have a few hours to marinate. Mason jars work well for infused waters. Leave the infusion material in the jar for a second filling of water.

You can make up your own flavors by adding berries, citrus fruits, and any other fruits or vegetables that you think sound good. Herbs are also very good in infused waters. My favorites includew basil, cinnamon, clove, dill, fennel, mint, and parsley.

GOOD MORNING WATER

To a wide mouth container of filtered water add:

INGREDIENTS

1 lemon, juiced

1-inch piece of ginger, peeled and thinly sliced

A few thin slices of lemon with rind

Honey to taste (optional)

Small pinch of cayenne

DIRECTIONS

Drink at room temperature.

SKIN WATER

To a wide mouth container of filtered water add:

INGREDIENTS

4 cucumber slices

2–3 mint sprigs

½ celery stalk, cut in half

DEHYDRATION

To a wide mouth container of filtered water add:

INGREDIENTS

½ lemon, juiced

3 lemon slices with rind

4 cucumber slices

2 mint sprigs

MELON COOLER

To a large container of filtered water add:

INGREDIENTS

½ cup honeydew melon, cubed

4 mint sprigs

½ lime, thinly sliced

WORKOUT WATER

To a large container of filtered water add:

INGREDIENTS

2 grapefruit segments

¼ piece green apple, thinly sliced

1 thin slice of pineapple

2 mint sprigs

· · · · · · ·

APPLE WATER

To a large container of filtered water add:

INGREDIENTS

½ apple, thinly sliced

½ lemon, juiced

1 small cinnamon stick

· · · · · ·

BASIL-LEMONADE WATER

To a large container of filtered water add:

INGREDIENTS

3 lemon slices

4 basil leaves

WATERMELON-CUCUMBER WATER

To a large container of filtered water add:

INGREDIENTS

½ cup watermelon,
cubed and seeds removed

¼ cucumber, thinly sliced

· · · ·

GENERAL HERBS

Add to a container of filtered water any of
the following:

INGREDIENTS

Just basil

Just rosemary

Just thyme

Just mint

Just sage

Just gogi berries

Using the Pulp from Juicing

Don't throw that juicing pulp away!

The pulp from juicing does not have to be wasted. Pulp can be used for making raw crackers, soups, stews, muffins, veggie burgers, and breads. Pulp can also be added to pet food or to make pet crackers. Salad dressing may be added to pulp and mixed with a salad or eaten on its own. If you have a garden, pulp is great for composting. Pulp can be dehydrated until thoroughly dried, ground into a powder, and used for a wide variety of dishes that may use savory flours.

If you don't have enough pulp after just one juicing to make a recipe, place pulp in a sealed container and store in the refrigerator until the next day when you juice again. Pulp will last up to three days stored in a closed container and refrigerated.

VEGGIE PULP BREAD

1 cup young Thai coconut meat

4 Medjool dates

2 cups veggie pulp

1 cup almond pulp (see page 185 for making
Almond Milk)

½ cup flaxseeds, ground to a meal

2 tablespoons lemon juice

Pinch or two of sea salt

Add rosemary, garlic, or any
seasonings of choice

Water as needed

DIRECTIONS

Place coconut meat and dates in blender with ½
cup water (more if necessary to make a smooth
but thick mixture). Place remaining ingredients in
a food processor and add the coconut mixture.
Pulse-chop until all ingredients are incorporated.
Divide mixture in half and shape into 2 loaves. In
order for loaves to dry in a dehydrator, keep each
loaf approximately five inches long and three inches high. Round the top of the loaves. Dehydrate on
a mesh screen at 115 degrees for 15–18 hours or
longer if necessary.

If using an oven, set the temperature to the
lowest number possible, place loaves on a parchment paper–lined baking sheet, and dry for five
hours. Keeping the oven door ajar will prevent
bread from overcooking.

VEGGIE PULP CRACKERS

Moisture in pulp will vary depending on the juicer used. Some pulp can be extra wet and others very dry. Adjust liquid in recipes as necessary.

INGREDIENTS

2½–3 cups juice pulp

1 cup light or dark flaxseeds, soaked in
2 cups water for three hours

1 teaspoon cardamom

1 teaspoon fennel seeds

1 tablespoon of any of your favorite herbs—
cumin, curry, Italian

1 tablespoon gluten-free tamari

1 teaspoon maple syrup or sweetener of choice

Sea salt to taste

1 teaspoon lemon juice

Water as needed to make mixture spreadable
and smooth

DIRECTIONS

Place all ingredients together in a food processor, including flaxseed soaking water. Pulse-chop to incorporate all ingredients. Taste and adjust for seasonings and adjust to your liking. Each batch might need adjustment depending on what vegetables were used. There are two methods for drying. If using a dehydrator, spread the mixture on a nonstick dehydrator sheet about ⅛ inch thick. If using an oven, spread on parchment paper. Score with a knife to create desired cracker size, as this will make it easier to break apart after they are dried. Dehydrate for two to three hours at 115 degrees. Or if using an oven, bake at the lowest temperature for 10 or so hours until thoroughly dry. Check often so they do not burn, and turn over once.

For dehydrator, when crackers are dry enough to turn over, place one dehydrator tray with mesh sheet on top of crackers, flip over trays and peel off the nonstick sheet. Return the cracker to the dehydrator and leave overnight or longer for a crunchier cracker.

Storage Tip

Store crackers in an airtight container. If they are completely dry, no refrigeration is necessary.

To make sweet crackers leave off the savory herbs and add cardamom, raisins, or dried cranberries, cinnamon, nutmeg, and a dash of sweetener of choice. Apple juice can be used in place of the water for a sweeter-tasting cracker.

VEGGIE PULP MUFFINS

INGREDIENTS

2 cups carrot pulp (approximately 8–10 carrots)

4–5 Granny Smith (green) apples

1-inch piece of ginger

1½ cups walnuts

¼ cup maple syrup or sweetener of choice

1 teaspoon vanilla

1 teaspoon cinnamon

⅛ teaspoon nutmeg

⅛ teaspoon allspice

¼ cup carrot juice

DIRECTIONS

Scrub carrots with a brush. Peel, core, and chop apples. Peel ginger by scraping skin off with a small knife or edge of a teaspoon. Juice carrots, apples, and ginger, and set ¼ cup juice aside for muffins.

Place walnuts in food processor and pulse-chop until blended. Add pulp to the food processor with remaining ingredients. Pulse-chop until completely incorporated. Remove mixture to a bowl. Mixture should stick together when pressed between fingertips. If needed, add a little more juice a little at a time. Taste the mixture and add more sweetener or herbs if necessary. Shape muffins by hand to desired size. Small ones take less dehydration time. If using a dehydrator, place muffins directly on mesh sheet for 12 hours at 115 degrees. Taste for doneness, a crust on the outside, and the consistency on the inside. Muffins can be dry or slightly moist, based on your preference.

If using an oven, oil a mini muffin tin with coconut oil and spoon muffin mixture into each compartment. Set oven on lowest temperature and cook for approximately thirty minutes or a little longer, depending on your oven. Keep the oven door open slightly and check the muffins often so as not to overcook or burn them.

VEGGIE PULP BURGERS

INGREDIENTS

1½–2 cups sunflower or pumpkin seeds, or a combination of both, ground to a flour

2–3 cups juice pulp (carrot is especially sweet and makes a nice-tasting burger)

½ cup onions, chopped finely

1–2 cloves of garlic, crushed

1 tablespoon herbs of choice

Sea salt and pepper to taste

1 tablespoon Dulce flakes (optional)

Water as needed

DIRECTIONS

Place sunflower or pumpkin seeds in blender and grind into a flour. Place the pulp, sunflower or pumpkin flour, and the balance of ingredients into food processor. Pulse-chop until incorporated. Scrape the mixture into a bowl and add water as needed to help bind it together. Taste and add more salt or herbs if necessary. To dehydrate, place the burgers on a mesh dehydrator sheet and dehydrate six hours at 115 degrees. Burgers can have a light crust on the outside and be slightly softer on the inside. For a dryer burger, dehydrate longer.

If using an oven, set to the lowest temperature and place burgers on nonstick baking sheet and cook for two hours turning once. Test for desired texture.

Veggie pulp burgers can be used crumbled up in salads, on lettuce leaves as a sandwich, or eaten alone with a sauce of choice.

More Cracker Treats

My daughter uses this recipe for a training treat for her little rescue dog, Bianca, but it's also perfectly edible as a treat for people as well. Lisa mixes juice pulp in Bianca's homemade meals, but a healthy treat for training was also needed. It's not always easy finding healthy treats for your precious pet. Processed foods are not good for us, and the same goes for our beloved animals. Harsh manufacturing practices used in making pet food destroy many of the original nutrients in the ingredients. In addition, many dog and cat products contain soy and corn, which are two GMO items that are heavily sprayed with chemicals. Why shouldn't our pets have healthy options too?

Bianca and all her furry friends love these cracker treats. Since you can also eat these crackers, be sure to leave some for your pet!

Herbs and spices are healing for humans, and many have the same effect on our pets. They can be anti-inflammatory and antibacterial, and can fight infections. You may use small amounts of these herbs and spices to flavor crackers. Check any additional herbs before using to see if they are good for dogs. Do not add salt to this recipe.

HERBS AND SPICES GOOD FOR DOGS

Cinnamon—good for dental health

Cilantro—good for dental health

Turmeric—antitumor, antioxidant, and anti-inflammatory

Basil—contains vitamins and minerals, phytonutrients, and antioxidants

Parsley—helps fight cancer, enhances organ health, and helps pass toxins

Rosemary—rich in vitamins, antifungal, antiseptic, and anti-inflammatory

Banana Up!

Add 2 bananas, one or so tablespoon of peanut butter, and a little cinnamon, which will make these crackers extra special.

BIANCA CRACKER TREATS

Use juice pulp made with ingredients that are not harmful to dogs. Carrot, celery, spinach, apples, and cucumbers work well.

INGREDIENTS

1 cup flaxseeds soaked in 2 cups water for one hour

6–7 cups juice pulp

¼ cup gluten-free oatmeal

1 cup sunflower seeds

1 teaspoon maple syrup or honey

½ cup water or more

DIRECTIONS

Place all ingredients into a mixing bowl and mix until well incorporated. Add more water if necessary for the mixture to spread well. Spread mixture onto a nonstick dehydrator sheet and dehydrate at 115 degrees overnight or 15 hours, turning once when they are dry enough to do so. Place a mesh dehydrator tray on top of the existing crackers and flip tray over. Continue drying.

If using an oven, spread mixture on a parchment-lined pastry or baking sheet. Set temperature to lowest setting and bake for approximately 45 minutes; turn them once and check often to be sure they do not burn.

ACKNOWLEDGMENTS AND THANKS

Over the past several years I've been encouraged by so many wonderful people around the world. Hundreds of letters and e-mails arrive telling me I inspired them enough to change their diets, when in fact they are the ones who inspire me to continue my work in helping others to get healthier. Every life that I may have helped change for the better comes with effort on the part of each person whose life was changed. I've received heartwarming letters from 11-year-olds and 70-year-olds with such inspiring stories. People whose health and lives are better because they took the steps and made the dedication to change. I thank all of you from the bottom of my heart.

Mike Mendell, my boyfriend of thirteen years, is a trooper beyond the call of duty. I introduce him as my better half, which is true. You know him through his photography in my last two books and in this one. You know him from just about every photo you see of me on my social media pages and my YouTube channel videos, and about every food photo you see that is posted on my social network pages. I know him as the best companion a person could have in this lifetime. Tirelessly he traipses across the world with me dragging books and equipment for my demonstrations. He is the kindest person and my great supporter.

To all my children, listed by age, not favoritism, which is a running joke in the family. They always sign e-mails or cards with TFC, "the favorite child." Thank you, thank you, thank you for all your constant love and support of everything I do throughout my entire life. Dan, Lisa, Jonas, and Mia you always make me feel special. I'm so proud of each of you and the kind of adults you've grown to be. You helped to inspire this book each time you asked for another juice cleanse recipe and for all your willingness to try every juice I've put before you. I couldn't ask for more loving children.

Grandchildren, all seven of them . . . lucky me! Beautiful, warmhearted, nonjudgmental, and all so kindhearted.

You help me stay youthful and current. Mackenzie, Hannah, Karly, Rocky, Luke, Audrey, and Gunner. My life is so much richer with all of you in it. I'm so proud of every one of you. Thanks to Toni and Gigi, my daughters-in-law, for always being kind and thoughtful and being such a great example to my grandchildren. My happiest times are when the whole family gets together.

Thanks to my agent, Kari Stuart, who always believes in my books and takes care of so many details to make them a reality. Thanks to Ann Treistman, my editor, for all her work in getting this book to look so beautiful and easy to use. Her input is always invaluable. Thank you, too, Countryman Press and everyone there who worked so diligently to put on all the finishing touches, and much thanks to my copy editor, Diane Durrett; great job!

Thanks to my wonderful longtime dearest friend, Julie Kavner, who always loves everything I do and encourages me in all my endeavors. Thanks to my dear friend Valerie Harper who is such an inspiration to me. Hugs to my friends Susan Santilena and Eileen Chousa Katzenstein and Michael Keller for all their support over the years. Thanks to my inspiring girlfriends who change the lives of so many every day, Cristina Archila, Victoria Davis, and Christine Mayr—for all your extra-special love and support and willingness to always be here for me. Your help with this book was invaluable.

It's good to have dear longtime friends in life like the wonderful Robin Leach who always makes me feel special and believes in my lifestyle and me. Thanks Stephanie Pross for your keen eyes, and Cindy Fuchser, Michelle Cerise, Mia White, and Kanai Dodge for taking time to test and taste juices. Kisses to my new friends Patricia Saint Claire of That's Amore in Mallorca, and Ami Beach and Chef Mark Shadle of G-Zen in Branford, Connecticut, who walk their talk and inspire. And thank you to the many special people who watch over me in the present and from the past.

INDEX